LONDON'S
HIDDEN CORNERS, LANES & SQUARES

Graeme Chesters

Survival Books • Bath • England

First published 2015

Copyright © Survival Books 2015
Cover Photo: Woburn Walk, WC1

Survival Books Limited
Office 169, 3 Edgar Buildings
George Street, Bath BA1 2FJ, United Kingdom
+44 (0)1225-462135, info@survivalbooks.net
www.survivalbooks.net and www.londons-secrets.com

British Library Cataloguing in Publication Data
A CIP record for this book is available
from the British Library.

ISBN: 978-1-909282-69-8

Printed and bound in China by D'Print Pte Ltd.

Acknowledgements

The author would like to thank all those who helped with research and provided information for this book. Special thanks are also due to Robbi Atilgan for editing; Peter Read for additional editing and proof-reading; David Woodworth for final proof checking; John Marshall for DTP, photo selection and cover design; and the author's partner for the constant supply of tea, coffee, food and wine (and for continuing with the pretence that writing is a real job).

Last, but not least, a special thank you to the many photographers – the unsung heroes – whose beautiful images bring London to life.

The Author

Graeme Chesters is an experienced journalist, copywriter, non-fiction and travel writer. He knows London well, having lived in the northwest, centre and southeast of the city, and is the author of a number of London books, including *London's Hidden Secrets, London's Secret Walks, London's Secrets: Bizarre & Curious* and *London's Secrets: Pubs & Bars*. Graeme is also a wine writer (and enthusiastic drinker!) and has written two wine books. He lives in Bexley in southeast London with his wife Louise.

London's Secrets:
PEACEFUL PLACES

ISBN: 978-1-907339-45-5, 256 pages, hardback, £11.95

David Hampshire

London is one of the world's most exciting cities, but it's also one of the noisiest; a bustling, chaotic, frenetic, over-crowded, manic metropolis of over 8 million people, where it can be difficult to find somewhere to grab a little peace and quiet. Nevertheless, if you know where to look London has a wealth of peaceful places: places to relax, chill out, contemplate, meditate, sit, reflect, browse, read, chat, nap, walk, think, study or even work (if you must) - where the city's volume is muted or even switched off completely.

LONDON FOR FOODIES, GOURMETS & GLUTTONS

ISBN: 978-1-909282-76-6, 288 pages, hardback, £11.95

David Hampshire & Graeme Chesters

Much more than simply a directory of cafés, markets, restaurants and food shops, *London for Foodies, Gourmets & Gluttons* features many of the city's best artisan producers and purveyors, plus a wealth of classes where you can learn how to prepare and cook food like the experts, appreciate fine wines and brew coffee like a barista. And when you're too tired to cook or just want to treat yourself, we'll show you great places where you can enjoy everything from tea and cake to a tasty street snack; a pie and a pint to a glass of wine and tapas; and a quick working lunch to a full-blown gastronomic extravaganza.

Contents

2. CITY WEST   67

Lovat Lane, EC3

Introduction

The inspiration for this book was the advice of the great Dr Samuel Johnson (1709-1784), something of an expert on London, to his friend and biographer James Boswell on the occasion of his trip to London in the 18th century, to 'survey its innumerable little lanes and courts'. In the 21st century these are less numerous than in Johnson's time, so we've extended his brief to include alleys, squares and yards, along with a number of mews, roads, streets and gardens.

London's Hidden Corners, Lanes & Squares takes you off the beaten track to seek out places that often fail to register on the radar of visitors and also most residents. Entries range from ancient history-soaked alleys and lanes in the City – where you half expect to bump into one of Charles Dickens's characters or even the author himself – to smart, pastel-painted mews in Chelsea built to house horses and carriages (now home to multi-millionaires); and from unexpected oases of Georgian elegance in traffic-plagued central London to tranquil Kensington squares, where you can hear birdsong and almost smell the scent of money on the breeze.

Samuel Johnson also said, 'It is not in the showy evolutions of buildings, but in the multiplicity of human habitations which are crowded together, that the wonderful immensity of London consists.' Every corner featured in this book has a story to tell, from those who lived there (actresses, bishops, painters, politicians, philosophers, writers… even ghosts of former residents!), significant historical events (from duels and demonstrations to plots and executions) and bizarre surviving landmarks such as a brick kiln, a sewer gas lamp and a Parisian *pissoir*.

Although this book isn't intended as a walking guide, most of the places featured are close to one another in central London – notably in the hubs of Westminster and the City, where you can easily stroll between them – and all are near public transport links and easy to reach.

I hope you enjoy discovering *London's Hidden Corners, Lanes & Squares* as much as I did, and if you happen across more secret gems on your travels, I would love to hear about them.

Graeme Chesters

July 2015

CHAPTER 1

CENTRAL LONDON

1. Abingdon Street Gardens & Old Palace Yard, SW1

Transport: Westminster tube

Also known as College Green, Abingdon Street Gardens sit opposite the Houses of Parliament, next to the elegant, understated Jewel Tower, with Old Palace Yard on the other side of the tower. This area is often ignored in favour of the obvious 'big-hitting' attractions nearby, but is well worth exploring.

Jewel Tower

Abingdon Street Gardens were laid out in the 1960s on land that once contained the medieval Palace of Westminster. The palace had two main courtyards, Old Palace Yard and New Palace Yard. Poet and 'father of English literature' Geoffrey Chaucer lived in the former when he was Clerk of the King's Works in the 14th century, and dramatist Ben Jonson had a house here too. Sadly, the yard and houses were lost in the 1834 fire that destroyed much of the medieval palace, with the Jewel Tower and Westminster Hall the only significant survivors.

The three-storey tower is surrounded by a moat and was built from Kentish ragstone in 1364-66 to house Edward III's royal treasure. From 1621-1864 it housed the House of Lords' records and from 1869-1938 was home to the Weights and Measures Office. It's now managed by English Heritage.

> The Gunpowder Plot was partly hatched in Old Palace Yard in the house of Thomas Percy. Guy Fawkes and his co-conspirators were executed here in 1606, as was Sir Walter Raleigh in 1618.

Gunpowder Plot conspirators

2. Albany Court Yard, W1

Transport: Green Park or Piccadilly Circus tube

Albany Court Yard is tucked away north of Piccadilly, near the Royal Academy and opposite Hatchards bookshop. It comprises a three-storey mansion and two service wings, with a courtyard in front. The buildings – known variously as Albany Court, The Albany or Albany – comprised a mansion, until being converted into exclusive bachelors' apartments.

Albany was designed by Sir William Chambers and constructed in 1770-4 for the 1st Viscount Melbourne. In 1802 it was sold and converted into around 70 chambers, sometimes called 'sets', for bachelors who weren't involved in 'trade' and who had good social connections; women weren't allowed here until later.

> Albany Court gets its name from Prince Frederick, Duke of York and Albany, who lived here in the 1790s.

It became one of London's most fashionable addresses, with famous residents including Prime Ministers Lord Palmerston, William Gladstone and Edward Heath; poet Lord Byron; authors Aldous Huxley, Graham Greene and J. B. Priestley;

dramatist Terence Rattigan; photographer and royal consort Anthony Armstrong-Jones; broadcaster Malcolm Muggeridge; philosopher Sir Isaiah Berlin; and actors Terence Stamp and Dame Edith Evans. Albany Court was also the 'home' of A. J. Raffles, the fictional gentleman thief created by E. W. Hornung in the 1890s. Today, you don't have to be a bachelor to live here, although you do need to be at least 14 years old (and wealthy!).

3. Angel Court, SW1

Transport: Green Park or Piccadilly Circus tube

Situated between King Street and Pall Mall, this is one of London's more atmospheric courts. It's narrow and paved, and takes its name from the 17th-century Angel Tavern which once stood here. Angel Court has covered entrances at both ends and on the corner with King Street sits the narrow Golden Lion pub, with attractive bow windows.

The pub dates from the earlier 19th century and attracts a mixed clientele, including tourists, office workers, and staff from the area's many gentlemen's clubs – plus the odd gentleman on the way to or from his club (open Mon-Fri, 11am-11pm, and Sat, noon-5pm).

A plaque in Angel Court, opposite the side of the pub, records this was the site of the St James's Theatre, built in 1835. It was demolished in 1957, despite an epic campaign of protest led by Vivien Leigh and Sir Laurence Olivier, whose heads appear on a panel relief above the plaque (below).

> The Oscar Wilde plays *Lady Windermere's Fan* and *The Importance of Being Earnest* had their premieres at St James's Theatre in the 1890s.

4. Bell Yard, WC2

Transport: Temple tube

Bell Yard runs north from the Strand, just to the east of the monumental Royal Courts of Justice building, very much in the heart of legal London. A paved passageway opening into a cul-de-sac, it's a narrow, historic thoroughfare with fine views of the Court building. The east side of the yard is lined with barristers' chambers and solicitors' officers, while at number 19 is a Law Society office (in a striking white building).

Bell Yard dates from the early 1400s and was the site of a tavern called Le Belle. This was demolished towards the end of the 16th century and later replaced by another tavern, the Bell, also now gone. Nowadays it's eminently respectable and affluent, but Bell Yard was described as 'a filthy old place' in 1736.

Carey Street runs from west to east at the northern end of Bell Yard and is the site of the convivial Seven Stars, a tavern popular with those working in the adjacent Courts.

Royal Courts of Justice

The Royal Courts of Justice is a vast edifice with over 1,000 rooms and 3.5mi (5.6km) of corridors, while the structure contains 35 million bricks faced with Portland stone.

5. Blue Ball Yard, SW1

Transport: Green Park tube

An unassuming, covered entrance connects Blue Ball Yard with St James's Street. As a result, the yard is often overlooked, which is a pity as the narrow entrance conceals a lovely space, once a stable yard and now the site of the unusual, two-storey annexe of the adjacent Stafford Hotel. The name probably comes from the Blue Ball Tavern on St James's Street, which was demolished in the late 18th century.

The yard dates from around the late 17th century, when it was probably home to the servants of the aristocracy who lived in the environs of St James's Palace. Back then it was called Stable Yard, as this was also

where the carriage horses of the royal family were kept. The mews-like coach houses, which today form the hotel annexe, were built in 1741-2 and later used as garages until being developed by the Stafford in 1990.

Today this old block is a notable survivor and retains a slightly rustic air, despite being in the heart of London's gentlemen's club land.

> Look out for the names of famous race horses displayed on the front doors of the hotel annexe's ground-floor rooms.

6. Bruton Place, W1

Transport: Bond Street or Green Park tube

Bruton Place runs from the northeast corner of Berkeley Square to Bruton Street. It's an attractive, L-shaped mews in a tranquil area of narrow streets and smart restaurants, built on land acquired by the 1st Lord Berkeley of Stratton in the later 17th century. It was originally the site of coach houses and stables for the grand houses on Berkeley Square and Bruton Street, while the name (also found in nearby Bruton Lane) comes from Lord Berkeley's country estate near Bruton in Somerset.

Bruton Place is narrow and quiet, with low-rise buildings on both sides and, although it now has various architectural styles, it retains a mews-like air. A couple of properties – numbers 36 and 38, dating from the 1890s – still have the hoists used to lift sacks of grain to the lofts.

Bruton Place has a number of places to rest and refuel, including The Guinea Grill, established in 1635, although its location is believed to have housed a tavern since the 15th century; it's now an outlet of the Young's brewery. Next door is Greig's restaurant, an upmarket grill in an attractive building.

7. Bryanston Mews West & Bryanston Square, W1

Transport: Edgware Road or Marble Arch tube

Bryanston Mews West links Bryanston Place with George Street, just off the southern end of the Edgware Road. It's a long, straight mews with a gentle slope, partly original along one side and with modern building along the other. Perhaps a little over-restored, it's still a quiet, civilised place to live in this hectic part of London.

There's a blue plaque on number 1 Bryanston Square commemorating the Turkish statesman Mustapha Reschid Pasha, while outside the garden railings nearby is a memorial to William Pitt Byrne, proprietor of *The Morning Post*.

The name Bryanston dominates in this locale, which is part of the Portman Estate and named after Bryanston, the Portman family seat in Dorset. The Estate originated with Sir William Portman, Lord Chief Justice of England, who purchased land hereabouts in 1553. Turn right from the north end of the mews along Bryanston Place and you come to Bryanston Square, rectangular and elegant, overlooked by terraces mainly original and in a variety of styles.

The central garden is private and features an attractive range of planting, including some large plane trees. The square was built in 1812 by David Porter and has featured in a number of novels, including C. P. Snow's *The Conscience of the Rich* and Algernon Cecil's *A House in Bryanston Square*.

8. Buckingham Street, WC2

Transport: Embankment tube or Charing Cross tube/rail

Buckingham Street is a short, historic thoroughfare tucked away off John Adam Street. It manages to pack plenty of interest into its modest yardage and claims to have housed more famous folk than any other comparable street in London, as a sprinkling of plaques attests. Many of the properties had different builders and are therefore in a variety of styles, so no bland uniformity here. Most have long been used for commercial purposes and some are listed buildings

Watergate in Victoria Embankment Gardens, which can be accessed down a set of steps from the street and across Watergate Walk.

> The Watergate (below) was the place where York House residents and visitors would alight from their river craft. It's now stranded well away from the river bank, showing how much wider the Thames was in the 17th century.

No. 14 Buckingham Street

The street was built around 1675 on the site of York House, one of the great medieval mansions that used to line the Strand. Indeed, the southern end overlooks the York

York Watergate today

The upturned cones attached to the railings in Buckingham Street are link snuffers. These were used to snuff out the 'link', a bare-flame torch made of hemp dipped in pitch which was carried by travellers in the days before street lighting.

The roll call of former residents reads like a who's who of historical celebrity. The plaque on number 14 states that 'in a house formerly standing on this site lived Samuel Pepys, diarist, Robert Harley, Earl of Oxford and politician, William Etty, painter, and Clarkson Stanfield, painter'. Number 14 was rebuilt in 1791.

Samuel Pepys also lived at number 12, from 1679-88 (moving to 14 afterwards). Philosophers David Hume and Jean-Jacques Rousseau lived at number 10 in 1766, while poet Samuel Taylor Coleridge lived at number 21 in 1799. Russian leader Peter the Great stayed at number 15 in 1698; writer Henry Fielding lived here in 1735, while in 1833-4 Charles Dickens occupied the top floor. The original number 15 was destroyed in the Second World War and later replaced.

The quirkiest aspect of Buckingham Street can be seen above the door of the house opposite number 12: an original fanlight window, which dates back to a time before a modern postal system. Until the 1840 invention of the penny post, houses didn't have numbers. Properties were instead identified by the name of the street and a copy of the pattern on the fanlight window above the door.

BUCKINGHAM STREET WC2

CITY OF WESTMINSTER

9. Carlton House Terrace & Waterloo Place, SW1

Transport: Charing Cross tube/rail or Piccadilly Circus tube

Waterloo Place leads off the Mall and is crossed by Carlton House Terrace, which runs to the east and west. Built in 1816 soon after the famous battle, it features several important statues, including one of the victorious Duke of Wellington astride his horse and another of polar explorer Captain Scott. The most eye-catching is the Duke of York Column (below), installed at the southern end of Waterloo Place in 1833.

Prince Frederick is thought to be the subject of the nursery rhyme *The Grand Old Duke of York*.

There's something slightly odd about the Duke of York Column. It's curiously tall – 124ft – and perched on top is a 14ft bronze statue of Prince Frederick, Duke of York (1763-1827), the second son of King George III. Frederick (below) became commander of the British Army and developed a (somewhat unfair) reputation for military dithering. He was undoubtedly feckless with money: when he died, he was a (then) colossal £2m in debt.

Following Frederick's death, despite his royal status, nobody could be found to fund a monument. In fact, the only way to raise the money (around £25,000) was to dock the pay of the British army for a day, regardless of

the soldiers' wishes. The great height of the subsequent column caused wags to suggest that it was the duke trying to escape his creditors.

Beyond the column, on the west side of Waterloo Place is the impressive cream façade of the Athenaeum, with blue detailing and a gilded statue. Founded in 1824, it's the most intellectual of London's clubs, named after Rome's ancient Athenaeum University. Opposite it is the Institute of Directors, which has been here since 1978 in a building that once housed the United Services Club. Founded in 1903, the Institute is the world's largest body representing individual business leaders.

Athenaeum Club

Take a stroll along Carlton House Terrace, built by John Nash in 1827-32 on the site of Carlton House. It comprises two lovely terraces, which the prominent architectural

critic Nikolaus Pevsner said 'may rank as the greatest terrace of houses ever built in Britain'; praise indeed. Number 11 has a blue plaque to William Gladstone, while number 1 has one to George Curzon, Viceroy of India (there's a statue of him nearby). Number 5 has plaques to Lord Palmerston and Charles de Gaulle (the Free French Forces had their headquarters here in 1940), while number 2 has a blue plaque to Field Marshall Earl Kitchener.

> Some noted institutions have their headquarters in Carlton House Terrace, including the Royal Society at number 7 and the British Academy at number 10.

Carlton House Terrace

10. Carting Lane, WC2

Transport: Charing Cross tube/rail or Embankment tube

Just to the side of the Savoy Hotel, linking Savoy Place and Victoria Embankment Gardens with the Strand, is unremarkable Carting Lane. Frequently clogged with delivery vans, it's worth a visit to catch a glimpse of London's only remaining sewer gas destructor lamp.

This quaint street light, lit 24 hours a day, was popularly thought to operate on human 'gas' from the sewers. As a sign on a low wall next to the lamp states (with mixed accuracy): 'The adjacent street light is the last remaining sewer gas destructor lamp in the City of Westminster. Installed in association with Sir Joseph Bazalgette's revolutionary Victoria Embankment sewer, which opened in 1870, this cast iron ornamental lamp standard with original lantern continues to burn off residual biogas.'

The Webb Patent Sewer Gas Lamp was invented in the 19th century to draw foul-smelling and potentially explosive gases from the sewers, and the one in Carting Lane did indeed once operate on human gas – and probably natural gas as well – but only until the '50s. Sadly, it now runs on standard fossil fuel.

At the north end of Carting Lane is a convivial Nicholson's pub, The Coal Hole, with an interesting selection of beers.

11. Cecil Court, WC2

Transport: Leicester Square tube

A historic walkway beloved by bookworms, Cecil Court runs between St Martin's Lane and Charing Cross Road. It has a decidedly antiquarian atmosphere and is home to vendors of antiques, memorabilia, prints and, especially, second-hand books. The court was first laid out in the late 17th century, although today's well-preserved shop frontages are Victorian.

The street has a varied history. A blue plaque on number 9 records that this was where young Mozart (aged 8) stayed from 24th April to 6th August 1764 during his family's 'Grand Tour of Europe' (they lodged with a barber called John Couzin).

A green plaque on number 27 recalls that between 1897 and 1915 Cecil Court was at

> Cecil Court's name comes from the time of James I, when William Cecil, Lord Burghley, built a mansion on the Strand. One of his sons, Robert, Earl of Salisbury, was granted land from Leicester Square to St Martin's Lane, and the court is still owned by the Cecil family.

the heart of the British film industry and was known as Flicker Alley. In the light of that, it's appropriate that the court has been cited as a possible inspiration for Diagon Alley in the Harry Potter novels, which were made into notably successful films.

12. Cleveland Row, SW1

Transport: Green Park tube

Cleveland Row is just off the busy junction where Pall Mall turns right into St James's Street, so is easily overlooked. It's named after the formidable Barbara Villiers, Duchess of Cleveland, who was one of Charles II's most significant and acquisitive mistresses. Charles presented her with Cleveland House in 1668 and she kept the property until the 1680s. The house, which was originally built for Thomas Howard in the 1620s, stood in Cleveland Row until being demolished in 1840.

St James's Palace

The row is surrounded by royal history. It begins by the entrance to St James's Palace (originally built by Henry VIII, although much of it had to be rebuilt later following a fire) and skirts the north side of the palace with its red-brick walls and characteristic tall Tudor chimneys. The thoroughfare narrows as it approaches Green Park at its western end, where it encircles Selwyn House. The architecture is more varied here; it's an attractive, characterful enclave and a throwback to a quieter, more elegant time.

Just off Cleveland Row, in Stable Yard Road, is Clarence House, which is the Prince of Wales's official London residence.

13. Crown Passage, SW1

Transport: Green Park tube

Crown Passage runs between King Street and Pall Mall, with covered entrances at both ends. Opposite the passage's southern entrance, on Pall Mall, is the entrance to Marlborough House. Crown Passage was built in the late 17th century and today is a narrow, pedestrianised shopping thoroughfare. It's very much what we think of as Dickensian in atmosphere – even though it's rather older – with original lamps adding to this impression, particularly after dark.

Towards the Pall Mall end of the passage is the old, characterful Red Lion pub (right), which reputedly holds the second-oldest licence in the West End. There's been a tavern here for over 300 years, although the current building is late Georgian. It has a frontage of black timber and leaded windows, while the small, cosy interior has dark wood panels, red upholstery and low lighting. The Red Lion is said to have once been a brothel.

Crown Passage is home to a collection of small businesses, bars and eateries, including a Davy's Wine Bar. Number 18 is the premises of a milliner and is a strikingly-attractive, Grade II listed building dating from the early or mid-18th century.

14. Dean's Yard, SW1

Transport: St James's Park or Westminster tube

At the west end of Great College Street, at the junction with Tufton Street, a covered entrance leads into the unexpected greenery of Dean's Yard. Although part of Westminster Abbey, this leafy garden square feels more like a village green, albeit one surrounded by important educational and religious buildings.

Among them is part of Westminster School, which was founded in the mid-14th century following a papal decree that urged all monasteries (in this case, Westminster Abbey) to support a school. It was originally a charitable establishment providing free education to the sons of local traders, but became independent of the Abbey in 1868 and is now one of Britain's most prestigious independent schools.

Former pupils of Westminster School include dramatist Ben Jonson, architect Sir Christopher Wren, actors John Gielgud and Peter Ustinov, politicians Tony Benn and Nigel Lawson, and composer Andrew Lloyd-Webber.

Number 18 Dean's Yard houses the School Office, while along from it are two arched entrances to the school, both of venerable age. Number 20 is the Chapter Office, and just past it is an entrance to the Abbey with multi-coloured gates. Number 3 Dean's Yard is home to the Westminster Abbey Choir School, while the south side of the yard is taken up by Church House.

15. Devereux Court, WC2

Transport: Temple tube

Devereux Court can be found just outside the gates to New Court Temple, and leads into the Strand. It's an attractive, paved court, quiet and small, the site of the Devereux pub. Both the court and the hostelry – and nearby Essex Street – are named after Robert Devereux, Earl of Essex (1565-1601), below. He was a favourite of Elizabeth I, but fell from grace and was executed for high treason.

Robert Devereux's son (also called Robert) died in 1646 and the estate hereabouts was sold to the infamous speculative builder Nicholas Barbon (c1640-1698); infamous because his often shoddily-built projects had a tendency to collapse. Barbon demolished Essex House and built on the land and, unusually, some of his buildings have survived to this day. Indeed, the pub building at number 20, plus numbers 23 and 24, are original Barbon structures, the first dating from 1676, although they were much modified in the 18th century.

> The Devereux pub (below) was a coffee house – called the Grecian – until 1843 and a bust of Robert Devereux gazes down from high on its front. Today it's a Taylor Walker establishment, open Mon-Fri, 11am-11pm, closed at weekends.

16. Ebury Mews, SW1

Transport: Victoria tube/rail

One of the lessons we learned while researching possible entries for this book was to investigate thoroughfares with the word 'mews' in their title. Further, we resolved to stop perusing nearby estate agents' windows, so as not to be slapped in the face by quite how far out of our price range mews properties are – their average cost adds new dimension to the term 'desirable'.

Ebury Mews is situated in a particularly upmarket area, between Elizabeth Street and Eccleston Street. It's a longish mews of mainly original properties; like many mews it's cobbled, albeit bumpily and unevenly. Across Eccleston Street it leads into the much shorter Ebury Mews East, which is similarly appealing, characterful and mainly original.

Nearby Ebury Street displays blue plaques to the composer Mozart, writers and bohemians the Sackville-Wests, actress Edith Evans and author Ian Fleming.

The name Ebury (the area also has an Ebury Square and Street) comes from Ebury Farm, an estate covering 430 acres that once belonged to Elizabeth I. In 1676, it became part of the Grosvenor Estate. Properties on streets bearing the Ebury name date, in the main, from the 1820s and later.

17. Exchange Court & Surrounds, WC2

Transport: Charing Cross tube/rail

Exchange Court is one of a few remaining narrow, atmospheric passageways linking Maiden Lane and the north side of the Strand. It has a wide entrance on Maiden Lane, the site of the Porterhouse pub, but then narrows considerably into a characterful passage with a real sense of age.

Heathcock Court is slightly further along the Strand, its narrow entrance is easy to miss and thus often ignored by passers-by. Bull Inn Court also connects Maiden Lane and the Strand, home to the cosy Nell Gwynne pub, which was built on the site of the Old Bull Inn, demolished in the late 17th century.

In all three cases, the term 'court' is rather misleading. It suggests width and airiness, but these are the opposite: narrow and dark, medieval and/or Dickensian in atmosphere, enhanced by gaslights. They're the type of narrow thoroughfares more associated with the ancient City of London than the West End.

In the 17th century, the Strand was home to a number of markets, and Exchange Court takes its name from the New Exchange market, which was opened by James I in 1609 and closed in 1737.

18. Gee's Court & St Christopher's Place, W1

Transport: Bond Street tube

A sign on a tall purple clock on the north side of Oxford Street (almost opposite Bond Street tube station) points the way to the entrance to Gee's Court, which leads into St Christopher's Place. And a sign is certainly required, otherwise the narrow entrance would probably be missed in the surrounding retail chaos.

Gee's Court and St Christopher's Place form an enclosed, paved and pedestrianised area redolent of London past, with tastefully modernised Victorian buildings housing a mixture of restaurants and shops, a number of them small independents. It's all very different from frenetic Oxford Street just beyond.

as St Christopher's Place. At the far end are the characterful St Christopher's Buildings, dating from 1877. Soon after, St Christopher's Place leads into Wigmore Street, with the historic Pontefract Castle pub on the corner.

> Once called Barrett's Court, St Christopher's Place dates from the 18th century. We owe its revival to Octavia Hill, housing reformer and a National Trust founder, who bought and restored it in the 1870s.

Gee's Court begins as a shoulder-wide alley before opening into a wider court (along with adjacent Barrett Street) and then narrowing again to continue

19. Goodwin's Court, WC2

Transport: Covent Garden or Leicester Square tube

Goodwin's Court is like a time capsule which whisks you back to the 17th and 18th centuries. It has a narrow, covered entrance on St Martin's Lane, almost opposite the Salisbury pub and easily missed. The court is narrow and uncovered, more an alley than a court, but well worth a detour. It's particularly atmospheric at night, when it's lit by the flickering glow of three large, functioning gas lamps.

Some of the buildings first appear in local rate books in 1690, as a row of tailors' shops. Although they don't have great architectural significance, they possess an intimate charm and atmosphere. The south side of the court is its glory, a row of attractive, late 18th-century, dark-brick buildings (many housing

businesses) with bowed Georgian windows, which hint at their previous incarnation as shops.

Look for the fire marks displayed outside some of the buildings. These badges date from the time before a public city-wide fire brigade, when it was up to individuals to insure their property against fire and insurance companies' fire-fighting teams would only tackle blazes at buildings displaying the appropriate badge.

> Not surprisingly, Goodwin's Court is popular as a film and television location and, like its near neighbour Cecil Court, has 'starred' in Harry Potter films.

20. Gray's Inn Gardens, WC1

Transport: Chancery Lane tube

The unexpectedly extensive gardens of Gray's Inn are an attractive, often overlooked part of legal London, comprising an expanse of lawn and trees. The gardens, sometimes referred to as The Walks, have existed here since at least 1597, when the records state that Sir Francis Bacon (1561-1626) – statesman, scientist and prominent member of Gray's Inn – was paid to plant trees here. The tradition has continued and the double row of Canadian red oaks seen today was planted to replace the substantial plane trees that were felled by the tail end of the hurricane that struck Britain in 1987.

Gray's Inn is one of the four Inns of Court, which are professional associations for barristers and judges. It's been established since at least around 1370 and takes its name from the family home (or inn) of Reginald de Grey, a Chief Justice who died in the early 14th century.

Seek out the entrance closest to Jockey's Fields to visit elegant Field Court, an attractive part of the Inn's buildings. Much of the Inn was damaged or destroyed during the Blitz, with successful, authentic rebuilding, and few original parts remain.

> You need to visit at lunchtime as Gray's Inn Gardens are only open to the public between noon and 2.30pm.

21. Groom Place & Surrounds, SW1

Transport: Hyde Park Corner tube or Victoria tube/rail

Just off Chester Street, Groom Place is a largely original mews, short and cobbled, with a dead-end 'dogleg' halfway along. It's lined with characterful, colourful houses and is also home to a narrow pub, the Horse and Groom, run by the Kent brewer Shepherd Neame and open weekdays from 11.30am to 11pm. It's small and cosy, with one bar and an upstairs dining and function room, while in summer there are tables outside.

> Beatles manager Brian Epstein lived around the corner from Groom Place (in Chapel Street) and is said to have met the band frequently in the Horse and Groom. This makes a change from the many London pubs that claim Charles Dickens as a regular.

Although close to teeming, traffic-heavy Hyde Park Corner, Groom Place retains its tranquil, village-like atmosphere, in common with the many mews in this area. Just across Chester Street is pretty Wilton Mews which leads to Wilton Street and its elegant terraces (Henry Gray, author of *Gray's Anatomy*, lived at number 8 Wilton Street).

The 'Wiltons' in the SW1 postcode (Mews, Street, Crescent, Place and Row) are named after the 1st Earl of Wilton, father-in-law of the 1st Marquess of Westminster, who owned land hereabouts.

22. Kingly Court, W1

Transport: Oxford Circus tube

Elegantly-named Kingly Court lies in the western reaches of Soho and is a courtyard surrounded by a mix of old warehouses and more recent buildings. It's approached by covered walkways from Beak Street and Carnaby Street; the latter entrance is diagonally opposite the colourful Broadwick Street Mural, which depicts some of Soho's more noted denizens.

> Once the beating heart of Swinging '60s London, Carnaby Street dates back to the 17th century and is named after a mansion that stood nearby.
>
> ## CARNABY
> ## STREET W1
> ### CITY OF WESTMINSTER

The vibrant courtyard is surrounded by three-storey buildings, with walkways on the upper two floors – it resembles an open-air mall (covered in winter), but one with an eclectic atmosphere. Restaurant tables cover much of the courtyard, while the surrounding tiers are occupied by independent shops, bars, eateries, art galleries and other small businesses.

Kingly Court and adjacent Kingly Street were built in the late 17th and early 18th centuries, although the court was later rebuilt. Much of this area was (and remains) Crown property, and until the early 20th century the court and adjacent street were named for the 'King'. The 'ly' was added to avoid confusion with London's many other 'King's' thoroughfares.

23. Kinnerton Street, SW1

Transport: Hyde Park Corner or Knightsbridge tube

An unusual and striking thoroughfare, Kinnerton Street is tucked away behind Wilton Place, a stone's throw from busy Knightsbridge. It was built as a service road for the properties on Wilton Street and Wilton Crescent, and its name derives from a Cheshire village close to Eaton Hall, the family seat of the Duke of Westminster, head of the Grosvenor Estate.

> This area is part of the Grosvenor Estate. Like Kinnerton Street, Motcomb Street is named after one of the family's properties, this time in Dorset.

It has a mixture of attractive mews houses and other buildings, and several small courts leading off it. These are now mainly private

mews (often gated), and include Ann's Close, Bowland Yard, Capener's Close, Frederic Mews and Kinnerton Place South. Kinnerton Street also hosts a couple of pubs, including the Grade II listed Wilton Arms, run by Shepherd Neame, dating from 1826 and noted for its external floral displays.

As Kinnerton Street approaches Motcomb Street at its southern end, it loses some of its character in a melange of more modern structures, although there are still some interesting offshoots to explore on Motcomb Street, notably Halkin Mews and Belgrave Mews North.

24. Lennox Gardens Mews & Surrounds, SW1

Transport: Sloane Square tube

Lennox Gardens Mews links Milner Street with Walton Street and is a wide, cobbled thoroughfare with some attractive architecture. Walking north from Milner Street, larger-than-average mews houses line the right-hand side, many painted in pastel shades, while on the left are the rear of houses on Ovington Street. The mews doglegs right and then left to reach Walton Street, in this attractive, upmarket enclave.

East of the mews, Lennox Gardens has some equally eye-catching residences. The gardens are lined by large, red-brick houses built by various architects; their general style was described by the art critic Osbert Lancaster as 'Pont Street Dutch' after similar properties in nearby Pont Street.

The land on which Lennox Gardens, the Mews and nearby Clabon Mews are built

Lennox Gardens Mews and Lennox Gardens are named after a trustee of the Smith's Charity Estate, the 6th Duke of Richmond and Lennox.

was part of the Smith's Charity Estate. Once known as the Quail Field, it was originally used for grazing and later as a market garden. In the 1850s, it hosted the Prince's Sporting Club, a cricket club that was a social as well as sporting success. At one time the MCC had its headquarters here, which closed in 1886 when it relocated to Lord's.

25. Little Turnstile, WC1

Transport: Holborn tube

Running south from Holborn towards Lincoln's Inn Fields, historic, narrow Little Turnstile is home to a number of small cafés and shops as well as the ancient Ship Tavern, which is on the corner with Gate Street. The pub was established in 1549 and rebuilt in 1923, as recorded by a plaque on the exterior.

Atmospheric and slightly claustrophobic, Little Turnstile has a distinct whiff of the medieval about it, which is highly appropriate considering its slightly grisly past. During Henry VIII's persecution of Catholics, the Ship Tavern hosted outlawed priests who conducted mass behind the bar. Lookouts were posted in the surrounding area and warnings sounded if the eager King's officials appeared, giving the priest a chance to secrete himself in one of several hiding places ('priest holes'), some of which still exist. The congregation would merely attend to their drinks, behaving like regular patrons.

Now a small, cosy hostelry with a wooden interior, the Ship Tavern features in tours of London's most haunted sites.

Some priests were caught, however, including some hiding in a tunnel in the cellar. They were apparently executed on the spot, and it's said that their screams can be heard to this day.

26. Manchester Square, W1

Transport: Bond Street or Marble Arch tube

Small, elegant Manchester Square is just north of Duke Street. The south and east sides of this well-preserved Georgian square have original, characterful terraces, while the north side is occupied by Hertford House. This partly red-brick mansion was built in 1776 and today is home to the Wallace Collection. The square itself was built in 1776-88 and named after the Duke of Manchester, the first owner of Hertford House.

Manchester Square has hosted some well-known residents and has blue plaques on numbers 2 and 3 – to composer Sir Julius Benedict and physician John Hughlings Jackson respectively – while number 14

> The Wallace Collection was mainly assembled by the first four Marquesses of Hertford, in particular the fourth Marquess, who left the collection and house to his illegitimate son, Sir Richard Wallace.

sports one to the statesman Alfred Lord Milner. Note also the original link snuffers outside number 5. In the centre of the square is a large, private garden, liberally planted with plane trees.

Most visitors come to the square to visit the Wallace Collection, one of London's best private collections of fine and decorative arts dating from the 15th-19th centuries, including such seminal works as Frans Hals' *The Laughing Cavalier*.

Wallace Collection

27. Meard Street, W1

Transport: Leicester Square or Tottenham Court Road tube

We sometimes think of Soho as a recent invention, dating back little further than the coffee bars, strip clubs and fashion boutiques of the Swinging '60s. But the area is much older than this and the name dates back to the 17th century.

Part single-track road, part pedestrian walkway, Meard Street is arguably Soho's most authentic and historic thoroughfare. Although it links two of the area's more prominent streets – Wardour Street and Dean Street – it tends to be overlooked. A pity as it's Soho's most complete original street, and feels more like Bloomsbury or Belgravia, with most of one side of the street occupied by a charming 18th-century terrace.

Look out for number 6, once home to the water colourist Thomas Hearne, as a blue plaque attests.

Sign of the times?

Meard Street was developed in two stages, between 1722 and 1732, by the carpenter John Meard, who also constructed the spire of nearby St Anne's church (in 1718). On the corner with Dean Street, opposite the Dean Street Townhouse (a hotel and restaurant), an understated plaque above the modern street sign, reads 'Meards Street 1732', a survivor from the second stage of the street's construction.

28. Mecklenburgh Square & Street, WC1

Transport: Russell Square tube

Mecklenburgh Square and adjacent Mecklenburgh Street skirt the eastern side of the green space of Mecklenburgh Gardens and, beyond, extensive Coram's Fields. Both square and street date from 1804-25 and take their name from Queen Charlotte (1744-1818), wife of 'mad' King George III, who was formerly Princess of Mecklenburg-Strelitz (a small German duchy).

The street is wide and airy, featuring handsome terraces of large houses, some fronted with brick, others with stucco and pillars, while the first floors have decorative cast-iron balconies. Number 21 displays blue plaques to the historian RH Tawney and the scholar Sir Syed Ahmed Khan.

Mecklenburgh Square is shorter, narrower and quieter, slightly tucked away in a corner. Numbers 43-47 form a terrace of attractive, original houses, with a plaque on number 44 commemorating the poet and writer Hilda Doolittle. Attached to the terrace is the mid-20th century William Goodenough House, which houses Goodenough College, named after Sir William Goodenough, Lord Mayor of London in the '40s. It stands on the site of number 37, where Virginia and Leonard Woolf lived from 1939-41.

Goodenough College

Mecklenburgh Gardens (below) are private, but you can visit for two days each summer during the Open Garden Squares Weekend (www.opensquares.org).

29. Mount Street Gardens, W1

Transport: Bond Street tube

Mount Street Gardens – tucked away behind Mount Street in elegant Mayfair – is a little-known, verdant haven in one of London's most upmarket areas. Both street and gardens take their name from Mount Field, which used to feature an earthwork called Oliver's Mount, said to have been built as part of London's defences during the English Civil War (1642-51).

The street was built in 1720-40 and rebuilt in 1880-1900, mainly in pink terracotta Queen Anne style. Today it houses a variety of chic galleries, restaurants and shops, while the adjacent gardens occupy what was once a burial ground which was transformed into this elegant, tranquil green space in 1899. The gardens are surrounded by some of the area's more attractive and interesting buildings, including the back of the Immaculate Conception church.

The gardens' sheltered, relatively warm location allows exotic plant species to survive, including a Canary Islands Date Palm and an Australian Silver Wattle.

Open from around 8am until dusk, Mount Street Gardens are a haven for bird life and local people, with rows of benches, shady London plane trees and some interesting features, such as the horse's head statue by Nic Fiddian-Green.

30. Neal's Yard, WC2

Transport: Covent Garden tube

This small enclave in St Giles, just north of Covent Garden, is named after Thomas Neale, Master of the Mint under Charles II, who developed this part of London. Neale designed the convergence of roads close to Neal's Yard known as Seven Dials, which, by the 19th century, was one of the capital's most notorious slums. In the 20th century, businesses began moving in and Seven Dials' fortunes rose in line with the redevelopment of Covent Garden.

Neal's Yard has narrow passageway entrances on Monmouth Street and Short's Gardens, which conceal a small, vibrant square with seating in the middle where

you can watch the world go by. Many of its buildings are painted in bright colours and house a variety of trendy cafés, wine bars and shops. The eateries tend to offer healthy foods, while the businesses include providers of alternative therapies.

In the '80s the yard was best known for Neal's Yard Dairy, purveyors of artisan cheeses (now located in Short's Gardens), and today is home to Neal's Yard Remedies, purveyors of upmarket lotions, potions and tinctures.

Neal's Yard Remedies sports a blue plaque stating, 'Monty Python, film maker, lived here 1976-87', commemorating the quintessentially British comedy team.

31. New Square, WC2

Transport: Holborn tube

A covered entrance off Carey Street leads into the impressively elegant New Square, which is part of Lincoln's Inn, one of London's four Inns of Court (the others are Middle Temple, Inner Temple and Gray's Inn).

Handsome, horseshoe-shaped New Square is worth taking your time to stroll around. It's lined on three sides with elegant terraces and has a garden in the middle with fountains: an unexpectedly large and airy space in the heart of legal London. The north side of the square features some of Lincoln's Inn's lovely buildings and gardens, also well worth exploring.

Some of the buildings date back to the 15th century but New Square is comparatively 'new', being completed in 1685-97 on land once owned by the Knights Templar, by barrister and sometime builder

Henry Serle. It was initially known as Serle's Court and wasn't originally intended to be part of Lincoln's Inn. It's said that Charles Dickens worked here for a while, in the office of the solicitor Charles Molloy, unhappily by all accounts.

The Carey Street entrance is protected by a large black gate (with an array of medieval-looking spikes on top) which is open from 8am-7pm on weekdays.

32. Pickering Place, SW1

Transport: Green Park tube

Pickering Place is a narrow, wood-panelled passageway off St James's Street, which runs along the side of wine merchant Berry Brothers & Rudd. Initially covered, it opens into a small courtyard: Britain's smallest public 'square'. A Georgian delight, the square is still lit by original gaslights and used to be a popular and suitably private venue for duels. The surrounding houses date from the 1730s, when it was known as Pickering Court.

A plaque records that from 1842-1845 a building here housed the legation (a type of embassy) of the Republic of Texas to the Court of St James's. After gaining independence from Mexico in 1836, Texas was a separate sovereign nation until annexed by the US in1846. Worried about interference from Mexico on its border, the Texans sought to foster international ties and established several international legations, including one in London.

However, attempts to curry favour with the British nearly backfired, because when Texas opted to join the US in 1845, the British wanted to keep it independent. The US 'won' and Texas became the 28th state of the Union and today is the second-largest after Alaska.

> Pickering Place gets its name from William Pickering, whose mother-in-law founded the grocer's shop that later became Berry Brothers & Rudd.
>
>

33. Pied Bull Yard, WC1

Transport: Holborn or Russell Square tube

Just southeast of the increasingly tourist-soaked British Museum, tucked between Bloomsbury Square and Bury Place, is a series of fascinating courts and passages. Together they comprise Pied Bull Yard, an almost hidden enclave of shops and eateries which resembles a smaller version of Mayfair's Shepherd's Market.

The area was undeveloped until the late 17th century and, like much of Bloomsbury, was mainly rural. Pied Bull Yard was part of the grounds of Southampton House and appears to have been known originally as Stable Yard. The current name was first mentioned in the early 19th century.

Today it's a pleasant, surprisingly tranquil and little-known escape from the surrounding frenzy of Bloomsbury tourists. Visit Pied Bull Yard for its specialist shops, independent booksellers – the London Review Bookshop is here – and interesting places to eat and drink.

The Dickensian-sounding Truckles (left), a fairly standard outlet of the Davy's chain, boasts one of central London's rare beer gardens. As a result, it's especially popular with local workers during the capital's occasional spells of clement weather.

34. Queen Square, WC1

Transport: Russell Square tube

Tucked away in a quieter part of Bloomsbury, this small attractive square is a leafy oasis with a lovely garden. Many of the surrounding buildings house medical institutions, while artist, designer and man for all seasons William Morris lived at number 26 from 1865-71, and had a design shop on the ground floor.

The garden at Queen Square (open 7.30am to dusk) contains a number of benches and makes a good lunch or people-watching spot.

The square was built from 1708-20 and the northern section of the garden has a statue of a robed queen which dates from around 1775. This was once thought to represent Queen Anne (or perhaps Mary II) but is now generally regarded as Charlotte (1744-1818), wife of King George III. Indeed, Queen Square was once called Queen Anne's Square and the current name is a neutral compromise.

On the corner with Cosmo Place is the Queen's Larder, a Greene King pub popular with those who work at nearby Great Ormond Street Hospital. The name is said to come from the above-mentioned Queen Charlotte, who used a small cellar at the pub to store food and medicine for George III. He was a regular visitor to the square to receive treatment for what was thought to be a type of insanity, now identified as porphyria.

35. Queen Anne's Gate & Old Queen Street, SW1

Transport: St James's Park tube

One of Westminster's most architecturally-significant streets, Queen Anne's Gate is notable for its regal buildings with their splendidly ornate porches, delicate iron railings, and interesting touches such as cone-shaped torch snuffers and elaborate wooden canopies.

> Queen Anne's Gate was originally two closes separated by a wall. The wall was removed in the 1870s and a statue of the queen now stands on this spot (see below).

16 Queen Anne's Gate

The street begins inauspiciously, opposite the Petty France entrance to St James's Park tube station, in the shadow of the ugly concrete Ministry of Justice building (which bears a green plaque to the philosopher and reformer Jeremy Bentham). But keep walking

to discover a group of attractive, slightly wonky houses (numbers 42-46) on the left. Ahead is an alleyway leading to Birdcage Walk, while Queen Anne's Gate dog-legs to the right to reveal a sweep of lovely, elegant terraces of mainly red brick in various styles, built between around 1704 and the 1830s.

A clutch of blue plaques attests to the street's popularity with the great and the good: number 1 commemorates Foreign Secretary Sir Edward Grey (note the carved wooden entrance); number 14 recalls antiquary and collector Charles Townley; number 16 has plaques to religious reformer William Smith and Admiral of the Fleet

Lord Fischer; number 20 remembers Prime Minister Lord Palmerston; while number 28 honours statesman and philosopher Lord Haldane.

There's a statue of Queen Anne (1665-1714) against the front of number 13. She was the last Stuart sovereign and reigned from 1702 until her death. She was plagued by ill-health and had to endure the heartache of conceiving then losing nearly 20 children, none of whom survived her. Perhaps that

> Queen Anne ascended the thrones of England, Scotland and Ireland in 1702. Five years later England and Scotland were united as a single sovereign state, thus Anne became the first sovereign of Great Britain.

pain survives, as her ghost is reported to walk the thoroughfare three times at midnight on July 31st/1st August, the anniversary of her death. Some stories make grander claims: that the statue itself steps down and walks around its plinth.

At its eastern end, Queen Anne's Gate leads into Old Queen Street, with more attractive properties. Numbers 9 and 11 are particularly notable, dating from around 1700 (most of the street's other houses are later 18th century) with blue plaques: number 9 has one to Richard Savage, Governor of the Tower of London, while the plaque on number 11 states 'A Building of Historical Significance of the William and Mary Period, c1690-1700'. Grade II listed, number 11 is also the former headquarters of the Beaverbrook Foundation.

Old Queen Street

36. Red Lion Square, WC1

Transport: Holborn tube

Red Lion Square leads off Procter Street, on the borders of Bloomsbury and Holborn. It was laid out in 1684 by the controversial developer Nicholas Barbon (c1640-98, see below) and named after an inn on High Holborn. Today, it's a mixture (some might say a mess) of architectural styles set around a pleasant garden (open from 7.30am to dusk).

One of the most interesting buildings is the Grade II listed Conway Hall (left), which formerly housed the offices of the South Place Ethical Society and is now the home of an organisation advocating secular humanism. It dates from 1887 and is located in a corner of the square, next to narrow, pedestrianised Lambs Conduit Passage, which leads to Red Lion Street.

Numbers 14-17 Red Lion Square form a characterful short terrace, with two notable former residents: Pre-Raphaelite painter Dante Gabriel Rossetti lived at number 17 in 1851, while the designer and all-round genius William Morris lived here from 1856-9.

> The square's central garden features a statue of anti-war activist and politician Fenner Brockway (1888-1988) striking a flamboyant pose, along with a bust of the philosopher Bertrand Russell.

Fenner Brockway

Strange though it seems, Red Lion Square was the site of one of London's most unlikely pitched battles. The square's developer, the above-mentioned Nicholas Barbon, was a man of many parts; economist, surgeon and speculative builder, notorious for his dubious land purchases and shoddy buildings. When the development was proposed on the 17-acre Red Lion Fields site, the lawyers of adjacent Gray's Inn objected to their country views being blocked by Barbon's buildings.

As well as mounting a series of unsuccessful legal challenges against the development, the lawyers took direct physical action, throwing bricks at the builders and fighting with them. They managed to halt the construction work, but not for long; Barbon is said to have employed some of London's hardest-bitten thugs to protect his builders, and the next time the lawyers tried to interrupt the building work, they were successfully driven off.

Only a few houses survive from Barbon's time and given his reputation, it's surprising that they do.

Peter Pan Book Bench (2014)

In 1974, Red Lion Square was once more the scene of disorder, when the right wing National Front was due to terminate a march with a meeting at Conway Hall. During attendant clashes with anti-fascist groups, a student was killed.

Nicholas Barbon

Bertrand Russell

37. Robert Street, WC2

Transport: Embankment tube

Robert Street is named after Robert Adam (right) and runs south off John Adam Street, which (you guessed it) is named after his brother John. The brothers were members of a family of prominent

Scottish architects who built the surrounding area. The handsome terrace of houses on the right of Robert Street (as you look south)

has a blue plaque that reads 'Robert Adam, Thomas Hood, John Galsworthy, Sir James Barrie and other eminent artists and writers lived here'.

Opposite, at numbers 5 and 6, is Adelphi, a monolithic Art Deco office building with handsome decorative details, including the crests for Manchester,

Leeds, Liverpool, Edinburgh, Belfast and Glasgow. It's named after the original Adelphi Buildings: a development of 24 neoclassical houses designed and built by the Adam brothers from 1768 onwards, taking in Robert Street and its surrounds. Numbers 1-3 are original Adam houses and are Grade II* listed.

> The four Adam brothers – Robert, John, James and William – were all involved in the Adelphi development: *adelphoi* is Greek for 'brothers'.

The current Adelphi dates from 1936-8 and has been described as 'savagely ungraceful', although it has been Grade II listed, so must have the support of some arbiters of taste. The main entrance is on Adelphi Terrace, overlooking Victoria Embankment Gardens.

38. St James's Place, SW1

Transport: Green Park tube

St James's Place leads off St James's Street in the heart of gentlemen's club-land. Built in two stages –1685-6 and the 1690s – by John Rossington, it's a classy, historic thoroughfare, with elegant terraces on both sides.

A number of plaques attest to some of its many famous former residents. A blue plaque on number 4 recalls that the composer Chopin left here in 1848 to go to the Guildhall in the City, where he gave his last public performance, while number 9 has a green plaque to Francis Chichester (who lived here 1944-72), the first man to sail single-handedly around the world by the clipper route.

Towards the end, the street widens into a small square before it doglegs right into a quiet cul-de-sac with a variety of architectural

William Huskisson is best known for being the world's first recorded railway casualty (in September 1830), when he was run over by George Stephenson's *Rocket*.

styles. Number 29 has a green plaque to Winston Churchill, who lived here from 1880-83, while number 28 has a blue plaque to financier, MP and statesman William Huskisson. The last building on the left (number 27) is Spencer House, a survivor from the time when London was full of private palaces.

Spencer House

39. Savoy Court, WC2

Transport: Charing Cross tube/rail or Embankment tube

Savoy Court runs south off the Strand and houses the entrances to both the Savoy Hotel and the Savoy Theatre. The Savoy is probably London's most famous hotel. Built in 1889 by the impresario Richard D'Oyly Carte with the profits from staging Gilbert and Sullivan productions, it has long been a favourite with the glamorous and wealthy. D'Oyly Carte also built the Savoy Theatre, which opened in 1881 and was the world's first public building to be lit entirely by electricity.

The name is six centuries older, for this was the site of the Palace of Savoy which was built from the mid-1200s onwards. Six plaques on the wall of the east side of Savoy Court describe the history of the Palace and site. The land was given by Henry III to Peter, Count of Savoy (the uncle of the Queen, Eleanor of Provence) in 1264. The palatial mansion built by Savoy became the home of Prince Edward and his descendants, the Dukes of Lancaster. It was reputed to be medieval London's finest mansion, though

Geoffrey Chaucer began writing *The Canterbury Tales* while working at the Savoy Palace as a clerk.

sadly it was destroyed in the Peasants' Revolt of 1381.

Savoy Court has a notable oddity: the vast majority of Britain drives on the left side of the road, but a Special Act of Parliament from 1902 requires traffic to drive on the right when entering Savoy Court from the Strand. For over a century, this has applied to all vehicles, be they horse-drawn or mechanical, and various explanations have been proposed for the anomaly.

It's said by some to be the result of the habit of the era's Hackney Carriage cab drivers to reach out of the driver's door window to open the passenger's door (which opened backwards with a handle at the front), without having to get out of the cab themselves, and/or because the hotel's front doors are on the right-hand side of the street. Other people think the explanation is more prosaic: to prevent cars that are dropping people off or picking them up at the neighbouring Savoy Theatre from blocking the hotel's entrance.

It's often claimed that Savoy Court is the only place in London where you must drive on the right, but that's not the case: at Hammersmith bus station, both the entrance and exit force drivers to the right-hand side of the road.

40. Sicilian Avenue, WC1

Transport: Holborn tube

Sicilian Avenue is an Edwardian-era shopping arcade – unusual, striking, a little bit over the top even, but often overlooked except by those who know it's here. The avenue sits where Bloomsbury meets Holborn, between Southampton Row and Bloomsbury Square. It was built in 1906-10 by R J Worley for the Bedford Estate, and was one of London's first pavement café areas. In summer it's a splendid place to watch the world go by.

Sicilian Avenue is a diner's delight and an architectural feast: it has classical Italian features, with pillared, colonnaded entrances at both ends and pillars running along the sides. The floor is paved and the decorative buildings on either side are in red brick with white terracotta dressings.

If you don't fancy pasta and meatballs (there's a Spaghetti House at the Bloomsbury end), try the Holborn Whippet pub on the other corner. Beer is the big draw here, with at least 15 craft offerings on tap, the range changing regularly, although the outdoor drinking area becomes very crowded during warm weather.

> The Holborn Whippet is so-called because 'the folk of Bloomsbury and Holborn parishes relaxed with a spot of whippet racing well into the 1800s'.

41. Smith Square & Surrounds, SW1

Transport: St James's Park or Westminster tube

Smith Square is reached from Millbank via Dean Stanley Street. Built in 1725-6 and named after landowner Henry Smith, it's dominated by the monumental St John's which was once a church and is now a concert hall. The Square's other main attraction is the smattering of lovely Georgian houses on the Lord North Street side.

Smith Square has had some very political residents. Both the Labour and Conservative Parties once had their headquarters here, Labour from 1928 to 1980 and the Tories from 1958 to 2003.

The eye-catching St John's is one of London's finest examples of Baroque architecture. St John the Evangelist was designed by Thomas Archer and built in 1713-28. At the time it was one of 50 new churches built under the 1711 Act of Parliament to serve London's expanding population; at a cost of almost £41,000, then a colossal sum, it was also the most expensive. The church opened in 1728 but was never popular. In *Our Mutual Friend*, Charles Dickens described it as 'a very hideous church... resembling some petrified monster'. It was gutted by fire during the Blitz and wasn't restored to its former glory until 1965-9.

St John's was once nicknamed 'Queen Anne's footstool', because when consulted about its design, the Queen supposedly kicked over her footstool so the legs faced upwards, like the building's four towers, and said 'build it like that'. The towers were also designed to stabilise the structure, which was built on marshy ground, and today it leans at a slight angle.

Adjacent Lord North Street (above) is one of London's best preserved Georgian streets and popular with Westminster's wealthier politicians, as it's just a short stroll from Parliament. It was built in the late 18th century as North Street and became Lord North Street in 1936. (Lord North was Prime Minister when America won the War of Independence.) It's been home to some famous people over the years, including socialite Lady Sybil Colefax, theatre producer Hugh 'Binkie' Beaumont, Prime Minister Harold Wilson and MP-turned-jailbird Jonathan Aitken.

> Some of the houses in Lord North Street still have painted signs pointing to their underground air-raid shelters.

Nearby Cowley Street and Barton Street are two well-preserved early 18th-century streets. Both are named after the actor Barton Booth, who had a house at Cowley, near Uxbridge. Cowley Street was built in 1722 and is still mainly 18th century; like Lord North Street, the houses are coveted by MPs. There are blue plaques to Director General of the BBC Lord Reith at number 6 Cowley Street and to writer and adventurer T E Lawrence at 14 Barton Street.

42. Star Yard, WC2

Transport: Chancery Lane tube

A narrow thoroughfare north of Carey Street, Star Yard is named after the Star Tavern that stood nearby. It was once open land next to the Bishop of Chichester's London residence, and was built on in the second half of the 17th century. Bishop's Court and Chichester Rents link the Yard with nearby Chancery Lane.

Star Yard is noted for two contrasting sites of interest. The first is a branch of Ede & Ravenscroft, London's oldest tailor and robe maker, established in 1689. It specialises in legal and ceremonial attire, and is where barristers and judges buy their gowns and distinctive wigs.

> The wigs used to be made from human hair, but now use horse hair, a technique pioneered by Humphrey Ravenscroft in the 1830s.

As the Yard narrows, it's partially blocked by a Parisian *pissoir* – a familiar sight in 19th-century London. Now Grade II listed, the urinal's exterior is a green rectangle of cast-iron, with latticing and attractive designs; the manufacturer's name (McDowall Steven & Co – Milton Iron Works) can be seen on one of the external panels, with 'Glasgow' below.

This very public convenience featured in an episode of *Rumpole of the Bailey*, when the late Leo McKern is seen to enter it, but it has been out of use since the mid-'80s.

43. Strand Lane, WC2

Transport: Temple tube

A covered entrance in the red-brick and terracotta Norfolk Building on Surrey Street (which leads south from the Strand) has an intriguing sign above it: 'The National Trust. Roman Bath. Down Steps Turn Right.' The doorway leads to a passage called Surrey Steps and, at the end, a flight of steps running down to Strand Lane, a paved, pedestrianised alley which, alas, sometimes smells like a latrine. Turn left and the lane takes you down to the river; turn right and you come to the so-called Roman bath.

The bath is a stone-lined hole in the ground, a plunge pool measuring 4.7m by 2m (15ft by 6ft), which is probably fed by water from the adjacent holy well (located

near St Clement Danes church). It's visible through a window in a wall and there's a National Trust sign providing information about its supposed origins.

The age of the bath is uncertain. Its brick design appears Roman but there's no record of it before 1784, after which it's referred to as the 'old Roman bath'. Charles Dickens mentions it in *David Copperfield* and the current view is that it's probably medieval.

If you want to take a closer look at the bath, you can arrange an appointment by calling 020-7641 2000.

44. Victoria Square, SW1

Transport: Victoria tube/rail

Victoria Square is a haven of elegance and relative tranquillity, a delightful discovery in the traffic-plagued area north of Victoria Station. It's a modestly-sized square, with small, low, cream terraces set around a paved central garden. There are around two dozen houses here, all Grade II* listed, some of which have large Corinthian pilasters rising through the first and second floors.

The garden contains a few trees and some shrubs and benches, as well as an attractive bronze statue of Victoria Regina as a young woman. Sculpted by Catherine Laugel, it dates from 2007 and depicts Victoria as she looked when she became queen in 1837.

Former residents of Victoria Square include author Ian Fleming and politician Michael Portillo.

There's a plaque at the base of the statue with a Latin inscription, which translates as 'Queen Victoria at the start of her victorious reign'. The statue – designed by Matthew Wyatt – is apt as the square was built in 1838-9 to celebrate the beginning of Victoria's reign.

At the square's junction with Beeston Place is a hotel, The Goring (above), which dates from 1910 and claims to be 'the only truly luxurious hotel still owned and run by the family who built it'.

45. Wilton Row, SW1

Transport: Hyde Park Corner or Knightsbridge tube

Cobbled Wilton Row is part of the Grosvenor Estate and runs east of Wilton Crescent and Wilton Place. All these Wiltons refer to the 1st Earl of Wilton, who once owned the land. Built in 1828-30, Wilton Row today comprises mainly residential mews properties, many rising to three storeys, with a variety of roof styles and many garages still intact.

Wilton Row is part of Westminster City Council's Belgravia Conservation Area, with consequent controls on any alterations to the properties. It's probably best known as the site of a pleasing pub, the Grenadier, which is at number 18 and is small, perfectly formed and allegedly haunted. It was supposedly built around the Duke of Wellington's officers' mess, but as the area was redesigned in the 1820s by Thomas Cubitt, this rather scotches that myth.

> As with many mews, the properties' original purpose was as coach houses and stables for nearby grand houses, in this case those on Wilton Crescent.

Outside the pub sports elegant red, white and blue livery, while the interior is cosy with a low, dark ceiling, panelled walls, original pewter bar and an air of gentility. It's said to be haunted by the ghost of a young subaltern who was caught cheating at cards and beaten to death by his comrades.

46. Woburn Walk, WC1

Transport: Euston tube/rail or Russell Square tube

Woburn Walk is an elegant, paved pedestrian thoroughfare, its entrance tucked away between an Italian restaurant and the County Hotel on Upper Woburn Place. It used to be called Woburn Buildings and was designed by Thomas Cubitt in 1822 as a shopping area. Both sides of the walk have attractive low terraces of well-preserved, bow-fronted shops, painted black at ground-floor level, cream above.

Antiquated street lamps and a few trees add to the character of Woburn Walk, which is decidedly Dickensian; this is reflected in the name of one of the cafés here, Wot the Dickens (the correct spelling, alas).

Woburn Walk is surprisingly tranquil, a quiet enclave in an area dominated by University College London and thronged with students. Walk to the further end and out into Duke's Road, which also has some striking buildings – look out for number 20,

A plaque marks the fact that poet W B Yeats lived in one of the houses in the block numbered 1-7, from 1895-1919.

with 'Middlesex Artists' above the elaborate entrance. From Duke's Road you can see some of the oddly truncated statues on Saint Pancras Parish Church. Owing to an error of measurement, the statues' midriffs had to be made smaller so they could fit their allotted spaces.

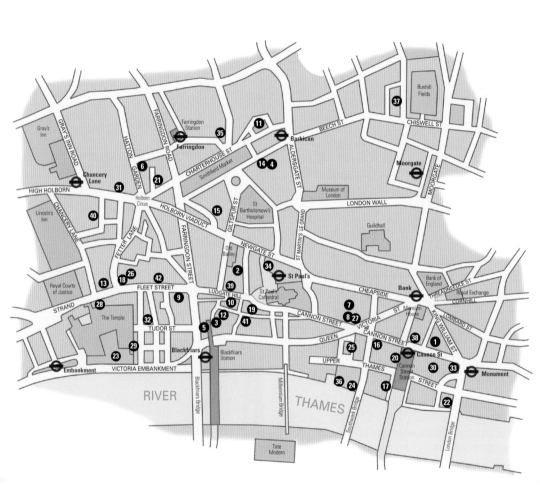

CHAPTER 2

CITY WEST

1. Abchurch Yard, EC4

Transport: Cannon Street tube/rail or Monument tub

Abchurch Yard leads off busy Cannon Street and is a slightly unexpected and tranquil cobblestoned area in front of the Guild Church of St Mary Abchurch, which is home to a number of watering holes. The name Abchurch might be a corruption of upchurch, to reflect the fact that the church was built on slightly raised ground and/or upriver from the larger St Mary Overie, now Southwark Cathedral.

There's been a church here since the 12th century and the yard was originally its graveyard. The current building is by Sir Christopher Wren and dates from 1686. It's noted for its lovely wood carving, some of which is by the great sculptor and woodcarver Grinling Gibbons – it boasts his only documented reredos in the City with the exception of the one in St Paul's Cathedral.

St Mary Abchurch has a shallow, painted dome and Wren is said to have practised here prior to perfecting his dome-designing skills on St Paul's; it's still regarded as one of his prettiest churches, with Dutch design influences.

The church wardens' pews are notable as they incorporate sword rests, as well as what are said to be dog kennels beneath the seats, apparently once common features but now rarely seen. A current church warden was sceptical about this when we visited, thinking it unlikely that people would bring noisy dogs to church.

2. Amen Corner & Amen Court, EC4

Transport: St Paul's tube

Amen Corner and Amen Court sit between Newgate Street to the north and Ludgate Hill to the south, just to the west of St Paul's Cathedral. They have suitably religious names for this area and are so-called after the prayers said by the medieval clergy of the cathedral during their processions around the surrounding streets. The same applies to nearby Ave Maria Lane and Paternoster Row.

Amen Corner is an attractive, peaceful, residential enclave where several of the doorways of the houses retain their Georgian

> The Campaign for Nuclear Disarmament (CND) was founded in Amen Court in 1958 in the flat of John Collins, then canon of St Paul's.

link extinguishers used before street lighting. Link boys were employed to walk ahead of residents lighting their way with a torch (or link), which were extinguished after they reached home (see page 22).

Adjacent Amen Court was built (reputedly by Wren) to provide accommodation for the

Amen Court

canons and scribes of St Paul's. It has a three-storey redbrick gatehouse to keep out visitors to this peaceful spot (it's private and belongs to the Cathedral) but you can peer inside and sometimes wander in for a closer look. The Court is a horseshoe shape and is lined with late 17th-century houses.

Unlikely as it seems, this attractive, tranquil court is reputed to be one of the City's most haunted locations. Behind the large wall visible through the main archway is a narrow passage known as Deadman's Walk. Condemned prisoners in the adjacent Newgate prison (demolished in 1902) were lead along it to be executed. Afterwards, many were buried beneath the wall and this is said to be the focus of the supernatural activity.

The most famous of the hauntings is by the so-called Black Dog of Newgate. This seemingly appears as a large, black, canine-like shape which can be seen slithering along the top of the wall, its presence accompanied by a nauseating smell. The Black Dog is thought to originate from an incident of cannibalism at the jail during a famine that marked Henry III's reign.

The victim is claimed to have been a portly prisoner, who was accused of sorcery. His ample, meaty frame proved too tempting for other starving prisoners, so they killed and ate him. He subsequently took the form of a dog to return to haunt his murderers and the place of his death.

Black Dog of Newgate

3. Apothecaries' Hall Courtyard, EC4

Transport: Blackfriars tube/rail

This courtyard off Blackfriars Lane leads into the airy, tranquil heart of the Apothecaries' Hall. It's painted a restful yellow and has a slightly ecclesiastical and scholarly atmosphere. The site once belonged to Lady Howard of Effingham and was purchased by the Worshipful Society of Apothecaries in 1632. Their first hall was destroyed in the Great Fire of 1666 and rebuilt in 1688 by Thomas Lock. What we see today is largely unchanged from then, except for some alterations in 1779 and 1927.

> Edward Jenner (1749-1823), pioneer of the smallpox vaccine, and Sir Humphry Davy (1778-1829), inventor of the safety lamp, were two of the Society's most distinguished members.

The Apothecaries were once part of the Grocers' Company but their specialisation saw them break away and they received their first charter in 1617. Although the word apothecary probably retains connotations of quaintness or quackery, people who pass the Society's examination are qualified as general practitioners and its membership is almost entirely made up of medical professionals. The term apothecary is ancient (dating back to Babylon in 2,600BC) and denotes somebody who formulates and dispenses medicines to medical professionals, the modern equivalent being a pharmacist or chemist.

Edward Jenner

4. Bartholomew Passage, EC1

Transport: Barbican or St Paul's tube or Farringdon tube/rail

Just north of Bart's Hospital on Middle Street a striking half-timbered Tudor gatehouse marks the entrance to Bartholomew Passage, which leads to the church of St Bartholomew the Great. As you pass through the gatehouse it's worth examining the other side, which retains a real sense of antiquity. It was built for Sir Philip Scudamore in the 16th century (restored in 1932) and the low door at the bottom left suggests an era when the average person was somewhat shorter than they are today. Mary Tudor (Bloody Mary) is reputed to have enjoyed watching executions she had ordered from this gatehouse.

On the left of Bartholomew Passage is a churchyard with several benches, while at the end is the church of St Bartholomew the Great (entry £4 for adults – with a café in the cloister where you can sample monastic beer!). The church was founded in 1123 as an Augustine priory by Rahere (one of Henry I's favourite courtiers) and boasts London's oldest wooden door, five of the city's oldest bells, and the font where the painter William Hogarth was baptised. It remains London's most significant Norman interior, with massive pillars, Romanesque arches and zig-zag moulding.

St Bartholomew the Great (left) has featured in several films, including *Four Weddings and a Funeral*; it hosted the fourth wedding, in which Hugh Grant almost married Anna 'Duckface' Chancellor.

5. Blackfriars Court, EC4

Transport: Blackfriars tube/rail

Blackfriars Court is located next to the Black Friar pub, one of London's most distinctive hostelries, and across the road from the recently renovated Blackfriars Station. It's a pleasant space with flowerbeds, trees, and places to perch, enjoy the sunshine and watch the world go by. But what we see today is only a corner of the original court, which used to extend further north.

> We're lucky we can still have a pint at the Black Friar, as it was scheduled for demolition in the '60s. It was saved by a campaign led by John Betjeman (poet laureate, later Sir John), a champion of Victorian buildings.

The court and pub are built on the site of a medieval Dominican Friary which gives the area its name; it was dissolved in 1538 on the orders of Henry VIII. The pub building dates from 1875 (the interior was refurbished in 1905) and is a wedge-shaped, Grade II listed construction. It's attractive outside – note the mosaic of its name – but inside it's nothing less than spectacular, with elaborate, sumptuous decoration that's a blend of Arts & Crafts and Art Nouveau styles. The pub's name is replicated in the decorative friars who feature throughout the building in a cascade of intricate friezes, mosaics, reliefs and sculptures.

6. Bleeding Heart Yard, EC1

Transport: Chancery Lane tube or Farringdon tube/rail

Bleeding Heart Yard leads off Greville Street, with the Bleeding Heart Tavern and Dining Room on the corner. A narrow, cobbled alleyway opens into the courtyard, which is home to several restaurants and small businesses.

Legend has it that Bleeding Heart Yard is so named to commemorate the murder of Lady Elizabeth Hatton, second wife of Sir William Hatton, whose family owned land around nearby Hatton Garden. Her body is said to have been found here in 1626, allegedly 'torn limb from limb, but with her heart still pumping blood'. The Spanish ambassador was a prime suspect, as she'd

> Bleeding Heart Yard has a Dickensian atmosphere, which is appropriate because it was home to the Plornish family in Charles Dickens's *Little Dorrit* – the novel makes mention of Elizabeth Hatton's 'murder'. Fagin's den in *Oliver Twist* was located at nearby Saffron Hill.

recently ended a relationship with him; after the break-up they were spotted together at a ball and she disappeared soon after.

But if a murder victim *was* discovered here it wasn't Elizabeth, as she lived for another 20 years. It's thought that the confusion arose because there were a number of Lady Elizabeth Hattons in the family. Even less satisfactorily for murder-seekers, some say the yard gets its name from a 16th-century inn, The Bleeding Heart, whose sign showed the Virgin Mary's heart pierced by five swords.

7. Bow Churchyard, EC4

Transport: Mansion House tube

Bow Churchyard is situated at the north end of Bow Lane (see page 76) and is a large space by City standards. The church that stands here is St Mary-le-Bow (below), about which it's said that only those born within the sound of its bells can call themselves true Cockneys. Legend also has it that the sound of these bells drew Dick Whittington back to London from Highgate to become the City's Lord Mayor.

The first church here was built 1080-90 on marshy land and had to be reinforced with bow arches, hence the name; the Norman crypt remains. The current church was rebuilt by Wren in 1680 after the Great Fire and the

The fine-looking gentleman (below) cast in bronze in the churchyard is Captain John Smith (of Pocahontas fame), New England explorer and early settler in Jamestown, Virginia, who died in 1631.

216ft (66m) spire is one of his best.

Take care, as this location has a history of calamity. In 1091, the wooden roof blew off the church and demolished a row of 'rude' buildings opposite. Two centuries later, the tower collapsed, killing 20 worshippers, while in 1284, a goldsmith was murdered here. In 1331, a balcony collapsed during a jousting tournament to celebrate the birth of the Black Prince, dumping Queen Philippa and her ladies-in-waiting onto the ground. The church was also damaged during the Second World War.

8. Bow Lane, EC4

Transport: Mansion House tube

One of the City's more attractive and lively thoroughfares, Bow Lane has been a public right of way for at least 700 years, although its current layout dates from the 16th century. Narrow, atmospheric and closed to traffic, it's a conservation area with a number of specialist retailers and places to eat and drink. At its southern end is Planet of the Grapes, a wine bar and shop with a few tables outside, which is a good spot for people-watching.

> This thoroughfare became known as Bow Lane in the 16th century. It was previously Hosier Lane and before that Cordwainer Street, named for the makers of hose (stockings) and shoes (made from soft leather called *cordwain*), some of whom remained in business here until Victorian times.

Bow Lane runs between Cheapside and Cannon Street, with the Guild Church of St Mary Aldermary on the east side. Aldermary is Old English for older Mary and signifies that the church is older than St Mary-le-Bow (see Bow Churchyard on page 75).

Large-scale development hasn't penetrated this area, which retains the atmosphere of the old City. It's well worth spending some time pottering around this charming, little-known segment of London, which is still characterised by small establishments.

9. Bride Lane & St Bride's Avenue, EC4

Transport: Blackfriars tube/rail

Bride Lane runs south from Fleet Street, near the attractively-tiled Punch Tavern. It's a narrow, curving, atmospheric lane, so-called after the Tudor Bridewell Palace. The palace was built hereabouts (on the banks of the Fleet River) in 1515-20 for Henry VIII and was named after a nearby holy well dedicated to the 5th-century St Bride (or Bridget).

> Bridewell Palace was the setting for Holbein's impressive double portrait *The Ambassadors* (1553), shown below, displayed in The National Gallery.
>
>

In 1553, Edward VI gave the Palace to the City of London, which turned it into a prison, hospital and workrooms, although it later became the site of a remarkable example of officially-sanctioned voyeurism. From the 16th century onwards, on arrival at the prison, inmates were routinely flogged, with 12 lashes for adults, six for children. By the 18th century, the sight of semi-naked prostitutes being whipped here had become such a popular attraction (in the days before reality television, of course) that a balustraded gallery was built for spectators. The 'fun' stopped by 1791, however, when the flogging of women was abolished. Many of the Palace's old buildings were destroyed in the Great Fire of 1666 and later rebuilt. The prison closed in 1855 and was demolished in 1863-4, except for the original gatehouse which is now incorporated into the front of an office block at nearby 14 New Bridge Street.

St Bride's Avenue is a narrow walkway, reached by six steps off Bride Lane. It runs alongside the church of St Bride's Fleet Street, which has a raised, paved garden concealing a wealth of City history: the remains of a 2nd-century AD Roman pavement and traces of the seven churches which previously stood here. This pretty church is one of London's oldest, probably dating from the 7th century. Set back from Fleet Street, it has an air of peace and is nicknamed the journalists' church, after the area's long (former) association with the newspaper industry. It's Grade I listed and has Wren's tallest spire (226ft), which was apparently the inspiration for the shape of modern wedding cakes.

St Bride's crypt is medieval and contains a museum with remains from most periods of the site's 2,000-year history, including a section of Roman pavement (at the back, raised above the level of the museum's floor).

10. Carter Lane, EC4

Transport: Blackfriars tube/rail or Mansion House tube

Long, narrow Carter Lane is one of the City's more attractive thoroughfares. It's old, probably dating from the 12th century, and runs past the original site of the Blackfriars Priory, marked by a blue plaque. This lane, and the several lanes and courts running off it, merit some exploration, for this is one of the most appealing parts of the City. And yet it's little visited, except by workers from nearby offices and trading houses.

The name is said to come from two 14th-century residents, Stephen and Thomas le Charatter, although – more prosaically – it may also derive from the fact that in the 13th century Carter Lane was used by carters taking goods from Fleet Street to the City. Today, it has a tranquil, almost village-like atmosphere, housing small businesses, cafes, restaurants, shops and pubs.

At numbers 36-39 is an unusual eye-catching late 19th-century building in the Italianate style. It's the former St Paul's Choir School, which is now home to the City of London Youth Hostel and is Grade II listed. Made of white brick, terracotta and plaster, it has unusual and important sgraffito decoration.

> Sgraffito – derived from the Italian word *graffiare* ('to scratch') – is a technique of wall decoration created by applying layers of plaster tinted in contrasting colours.

11. Charterhouse Square, EC1

Transport: Barbican tube or Farringdon tube/rail

Charterhouse Square is a large, airy space in Clerkenwell, named after the Carthusian monastery founded here in 1371. The square has Tudor, Georgian, Victorian and Art Deco buildings, and is built on the site of London's largest plague pit where some 50,000 victims of the Black Death were buried between 1348 and the early 15th century,

Gates prevent vehicles entering the square from Charterhouse Street, and just past them is the arched entrance to Sutton's Hospital (below) in Charterhouse. In 1611 the property here was bought by Thomas Sutton, an Elizabethan merchant and adventurer, and became a home for poor gentlemen (a sort of almshouse) and a famous school, Charterhouse School. The school moved to Surrey in 1872. Today the property is part

> In 2013, excavations for London's Crossrail project unearthed 25 skeletons from the mid-14th century under Charterhouse Square. DNA analysis revealed interesting data about their diet, health and occupations.

of the campus of Queen Mary University of London, and lodgings are still kept for gentlemen who fall on hard times.

Further around Charterhouse Square is the striking Florin Court, with its impressive, undulating facade. This '30s Art Deco residential building was used as the fictional home of Hercule Poirot in the long-running television series based on Agatha Christie's novels (it was renamed Whitehaven Mansions in the series).

12. Church Entry, EC4

Transport: Blackfriars tube/rail

Church Entry is a narrow passageway off Carter Lane (see page 79) which links with Ireland Yard and Playhouse Yard in a part of the City that's redolent of medieval times. The name commemorates two churches: the church of the Blackfriars Priory, which was founded in 1278 and dissolved in 1538 by Henry VIII, and St Ann Blackfriars, which was consecrated in 1597 and destroyed in 1666 by the Great Fire; it wasn't rebuilt and the parish was united with that of St Andrew by the Wardrobe.

The Vestry Hall is Grade II listed and was built by Bannister Fletcher and Sons in 1905, with a façade in the Edwardian Baroque style. Bannister Fletcher was the author of the noted *History of Architecture*.

Church Entry has two interesting sights. It's home to the petite, decorative St Ann's Vestry Hall (right), which hosts two organisations: the Ancient Monuments Society and the poignantly-named Friends of Friendless Churches.

Opposite the hall is a small courtyard garden, St Ann Blackfriars Burial Grounds, which is built on the remains of the nave of Blackfriars Priory church. It's enclosed and shaded, with some shrubs and seating (open 8am-7pm or dusk, if earlier), and is a slightly melancholy spot.

13. Clifford's Inn Passage, EC4

Transport: Chancery Lane or Temple tube

The entrance to Clifford's Inn Passage is between 187 and 188 Fleet Street. It's a narrow walkway and the name is evidence that London used to have more Inns of Court and Chancery than the remaining four (Gray's Inn, Lincoln's Inn, Middle Temple and Inner Temple). The former gatehouse – a small, arched structure – is the only survivor of an Inn that existed for around 550 years.

Clifford's Inn Passage was home to some well-known residents. The writers Leonard and Virginia Woolf lived here in 1912-13.

Clifford's Inn Passage leads to the rear of the Maughan Library, which is part of King's College, London. There's not much else to see in the passage, but it's atmospheric and the associated history is interesting. The name comes from Robert Clifford, who owned land and a house here in 1307, before the area became a centre for the legal profession. When he died his family leased the property to some law students.

Initially known as Clifford's House, it became Clifford's Inn from around 1345 and was the first of the Inns of Chancery,

although the freehold didn't officially transfer to the Inn until 1618. It ceased functioning as an Inn in 1862.

Maughan Library

14. Cloth Court, Cloth Fair & East Passage, EC1

Transport: Barbican tube

Cloth Fair leads off West Smithfield, just past Bartholomew Passage (see page 72), and Cloth Court leads off Cloth Fair. For centuries this area was home to cloth merchants and drapers, while the 'fair' in the name refers to the noted Bartholomew Fair, which was held annually at adjacent Smithfield from 1133-1855 and was once England's main cloth fair.

On the corner of Cloth Fair and Cloth Court, looking like something from a film set, handsome 41/42 Cloth Fair (right) is a notable survivor. It's the City's oldest house, built 1597-1614, and the only one to survive 1666's Great Fire. Originally part of a larger grouping of 11 houses with a courtyard in the middle – called The Square in Launders Green – the building escaped the worst of the fire because it was enclosed by a large set of priory walls.

Ironically, it was nearly lost a second time, in 1929, when it was deemed a dangerous structure by the City of London Corporation and earmarked for demolition. Luckily the house was saved and today is Grade II* listed. It isn't open to the public, which perhaps is just as well, as there are rumoured to be skeletons in the foundations and ghostly inhabitants!

A set of leaded windows at 41/42 Cloth Fair carries the signatures (etched with a diamond pen) of some notable visitors, including the Queen Mother, Viscount Montgomery of Alamein and Sir Winston Churchill.

It's appropriate that the poet Sir John Betjeman, a noted campaigner to save historic buildings, lived at 43/44 Cloth Court for a time. Cloth Court does a dogleg and leads into Rising Sun Court, named after a pub, in this charming maze of medieval alleys and passageways.

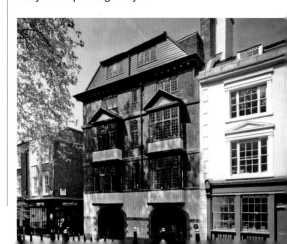

Back on Cloth Fair, the road runs along the side of St Bartholomew the Great Church (see Bartholomew Passage on page 72), offering a good view of the interesting variety of styles (and eras) represented in this ancient building's construction. The Founders' Hall is at 1 Cloth Fair, beyond the church. It dates only from the '80s, although the company originated in the 14th century and its first hall was built in 1531, on Lothbury.

As Cloth Fair becomes Middle Street, East Passage leads off it next to a sign for a pub, the Old Red Cow. The passage is narrow and full of character, and feels half-forgotten in this intriguing corner of the City.

The Worshipful Company of Founders (to use its full title) was comprised of artisans who cast items in brass and bronze.

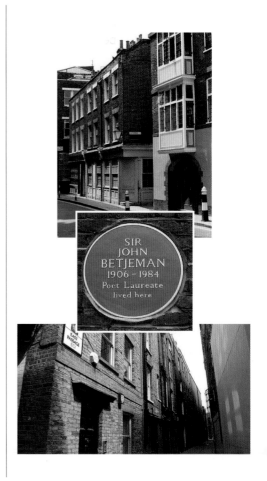

SIR
JOHN
BETJEMAN
1906 – 1984
Poet Laureate
lived here

15. Cock Lane, EC1

Transport: Farringdon tube/rail or St Paul's tube

Cock Lane connects Giltspur Street and Snow Hill, and is mainly lined with neutral, modern buildings, but manages to retain some character and has a past rich in fable and fact. It might seem probable that this suggestively-named street is so-called because it was once the site of a poultry market or chicken farm. But what in medieval times was called Cokkes Lane actually derives its name from the frank fact that it was one of the few places – perhaps the only place – in 14th-century London where brothels were legal. So hope lingers for the mucky-minded.

> Cock Lane was, somewhat inappropriately, where John Bunyan – Christian preacher and author of *The Pilgrim's Progress* (said to be England's first best-seller) – died from a fever in 1688.

The junction of Cock Lane and Giltspur Street (the latter so-called because gilt spurs were made here) is known as Pye Corner and marks the westernmost extent of the Great Fire of 1666. This is commemorated by the eye-catching, gilt cherub known as the Golden Boy of Pye Corner, set high on the wall. It was originally built on the front of a pub called The Fortune of War, which was demolished in 1910. The cherub is supposed to be plump to reinforce the moralistic idea that the Great Fire was sent to punish Londoners for their gluttony (it began and ended at food-related locations, Pudding Lane and Pye Corner). In these well-fed times, however, he doesn't appear especially well-nourished.

Tile & terracotta shop-front

The haunted building

Cock Lane was also the site of the so-called Cock Lane Ghost – delightfully nicknamed 'Scratching Fanny' – which manifested itself in 1762. It attracted mass public attention, and was also a focus for a contemporary religious controversy between Methodists and orthodox Anglicans concerning a spiritual afterlife.

A commission (which included the Duke of York and Samuel Johnson) was set up to investigate the supposed haunting and concluded that it was a fraud. Many people had queued and paid to ask questions of a girl, Elizabeth Parsons, who was said to make contact with a deceased young woman called Fanny. The perpetrator – Elizabeth's father, Richard Parsons – was subsequently pilloried and imprisoned. Surprisingly, he was kindly treated by the people he had tried to fool, being showered with small change in the pillory rather than the usual rotten fruit and vegetables.

The Cock Lane Ghost was immortalised in two of William Hogarth's satirical drawings and even got a name check a century later in some of Charles Dickens' works.

16. College Hill, EC4

Transport: Cannon Street tube/rail

There's plenty of character and history in this short thoroughfare, which has several connections with Dick Whittington – 15th-century merchant, Member of Parliament, Lord Mayor of London (four times) and Sheriff of London. The Hill derives its name from the College of St Spirit and St Mary that Whittington founded within the church of St Michael Paternoster Royal to ensure that his soul would go to heaven.

Numbers 21 and 23 boast fine decorative entrances: 17th-century stone doorcases that lead into an attractive 18th-century frontage. The Hill also boasts four blue plaques: at number 4, which marks the Duke of Buckingham's house in 1672; numbers 19 and 20, which were Dick Whittington's home in the 1420s; number 23, which was the second Turners' Hall; and at the bottom of the hill on St Michael Paternoster Royal, which was rebuilt by Whittington and is where he's buried.

The church's entrance is on adjacent College Street and displays its Dick Whittington connection with a modern stained-glass window (right) of a contemporary-looking Dick and his cat. The church is also the base of the Mission to Seafarers.

The Royal in the church's name is a corruption of Reole, the name of a nearby street that housed merchants who imported wine from La Reole near Bordeaux.

St Michael Paternoster Royal

17. Cousin Lane & Steelyard Passage, EC4

Transport: Cannon Street tube/rail

Cousin Lane runs alongside Cannon Street Station, from Upper Thames Street to the river. It's said to be named after a William Cousin, who lived here during Richard II's reign (1377-99). At the bottom is a Fullers pub, The Banker, with a small terrace and steps leading down to the Thames.

Just before the pub a left turn takes you into Steelyard Passage, a slightly creepy walkway that runs under the station. Now part of the Thames Path, it's also a reminder

of the area's Germanic past. This was once the London base of the Hanseatic League, a group of German ports that banded together into a trading league and later incorporated ports along much of the Baltic and North Sea coasts. The Steelyard refers to the large scales that were used by the League to weigh imported goods; nearby Hanseatic Walk also recalls this mighty coalition.

It's thought that the League was based here from as early as the 12th century; the Steelyard was destroyed by the Great Fire but was partly rebuilt and German merchants operated here until 1853. In 1865, Cannon Street Station was built on the site.

Cousin Lane features two mounted cannons (right), which face away from Cannon Street station. Strangely, the name doesn't come from cannon-makers but from candle-makers – in 1190 its name was Candelwrichstrete Street – the original residents of Cannon Street.

18. Crane Court, EC4

Transport: Blackfriars tube/rail

Crane Court is near the junction of Fleet Street and Fetter Lane. L-shaped and atmospheric, it's another reminder of what olde London was like and is the type of place where you half expect to bump into one of Charles Dickens's characters.

> Like many London streets, Crane Court takes its name from a tavern, The Two Cranes, which once stood on this site.

First mentioned in 1662, Crane Court was destroyed – and rebuilt – after the Great Fire which took place four years later. The famous (or infamous), 17th-century speculative builder Nicholas Barbon owned a couple of properties here – numbers 5 and 6 – which alas burned down in 1971. They were London's oldest-known post-1666 houses and the earliest examples of Barbon's work.

The Royal Society had its first headquarters in the court, from 1710, moving to Somerset House in 1780; Newton was a regular attendee (he was the Society's President). The satirical magazine *Punch* was first printed in Crane Court in 1841 (at number 9) and *The Illustrated London News* in 1842 (at number 10). So the thoroughfare has played a significant part in London's scientific and cultural history, yet most people haven't heard of it, let alone visited. Atmosphere and history are its main draws today.

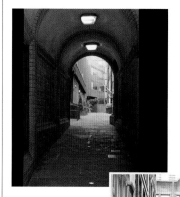

19. Dean's Court, EC4

Transport: St Paul's tube

A short street linking St Paul's Cathedral with Carter Lane, Dean's Court is attractive but often overlooked, being in the shadow of one of London's most visited attractions. But it's well worth seeking out – take the turning next to the striking, Italianate City of London Youth Hostel (see Carter Lane on page 79) – not least for its ecclesiastical connections.

> The Bishop of London is the Church of England's third most senior figure, after the Archbishops of Canterbury and York.

Map of the Old Deanery

This notably secluded street gets its name from the attractive redbrick Old Deanery, set behind a wall in a modestly-sized, cobbled courtyard guarded by some splendid trees. It was built in 1670 as the residence of the Dean of nearby St Paul's and is the work of Sir Christopher Wren; there's a slight Dutch influence in its understated and elegant design.

The Old Deanery (left) is now the palace of the Bishop of London, whose London residence was Fulham Palace on the banks of the Thames in west London for over a millennium. Since 1995, the office has been held by the Right Reverend and Right Honourable Richard Charters, the 132nd Bishop of London.

20. Dowgate Hill, EC4

Transport: Cannon Street tube/rail

Dowgate Hill runs south along one side of Cannon Street Station and is invariably ignored by commuters. It's named after a water gate near where the Walbrook entered the Thames, and from the 12th century was known as Dunegate or Doungate.

Three of the City's Livery Companies have their halls on the hill. Number 4 is home to the Tallow Chandlers' Hall, attractive and slightly camp, with gilt angels over the door. Peer inside, if you can, for a glimpse of authentic late 17th-century London. The company's name refers to the tallow candles used for lighting. It received its first charter in 1462 and its hall has been here since 1476, though the current building dates from 1672.

A gated entrance at number 8.5 (not a misprint) leads to the Skinners' Hall. If it's open, you can see the pretty courtyard within. The company received its first charter in 1327 and the hall has probably been on this site since 1380. The current building is Grade I listed and dates from 1670, the frontage from 1778.

Finally, at number 10 is the Dyers' Hall. The building dates from 1842, and is the third location for the Dyers Guild, which dates back to 1188.

The Worshipful Company of Dyers shares an unusual privilege with that of the Vintners: they are the only two guilds permitted to keep swans on the Thames.

Tallow Chandlers' Hall

Skinners' Hall

Dyers Guild Coat of Arms

21. Ely Place & Ely Court, EC1

Transport: Chancery Lane tube or Farringdon tube/rail

Ely Place is an attractive Georgian cul-de-sac off Charterhouse Street. It's a Crown property, which means it officially belongs to the Queen. As such, it isn't part of the City of London and is exempt from the authority of the Lord Mayor. It remains a private road and is protected at its southern end by a small gatehouse, guarded by a ceremonial officer called a beadle, while at its northern end, a wooden door leads into the Bleeding Heart Restaurant (see Bleeding Heart Yard on page 74).

Ely Place was the site of the Bishop of Ely's London residence from the end of the 13th century until 1772. The grounds covered 58 acres, stretching down to the Thames, and included lawns, orchards, ponds, strawberry fields and vineyards. The

> The Bishops' strawberries were reputedly the finest in London and are mentioned in Shakespeare's *Richard III*.

Saint Etheldreda

dilapidated palace was demolished in the late 18th century and replaced by the elegant brick terraces that now line the street. The adjoining ancient church of St Etheldreda's (once the Bishops' chapel) still stands proud between one of the Georgian terraces and Audrey House.

St Etheldreda's is Britain's oldest existing Catholic church, built in 1250-90 on the site of an earlier structure and named after the 7th-century Abbess of Ely; it's said that part of her hand is stored by the high altar. The church has an unusual layout, partly subterranean, and conveys a real sense of age and mystery. The crypt dates to around 1250 and incorporates much older walls, which may be part of a Roman basilica.

Ely Court is a narrow passage to the left of Ely Place (with your back to the gatehouse), narrow and covered at the ends, widening slightly in the middle, and home to a quaint, atmospheric pub. Ye Olde Mitre (Mon-Fri, 11am-11pm) is one of London's oldest taverns. It dates back to 1547, although the current building, with its oak front and opaque leaded windows, is from the 1770s, built shortly after the demolition of the Bishops' palace. The Old Mitre used to have a reputation as a difficult pub to find, although nowadays there are large signs at both ends of Ely Place.

> Although the pub sits at the geographical heart of London, until recently it was deemed to be a part of Cambridgeshire (where Ely is located). As a result, criminals could lay low here and in the surrounding alleyways, which were beyond the reach of London's law officers.

22. Fishmongers' Hall Wharf, EC4

Transport: Monument tube

Tucked just west of London Bridge on the north bank of the Thames, Fishmongers' Hall Wharf lies in front of the eponymous hall. This wide space is part of the Thames Path and there are impressive views of the Shard rising behind London Bridge Station and of HMS Belfast along the river to the east.

Fishmongers' Hall is home to the Fishmongers' Livery Company, one of the few that still performs its original function. The first hall was erected in 1310, while the second, which was built on the present site, was bequeathed to the company in 1434 and lost in the Great Fire. The current building dates from 1834.

Fish had a religious significance in the medieval diet which made the Fishmongers' Company wealthy and influential. Among its riches is a fine collection of 17th- and 18th-century silver plate, as well as the dagger with which Lord Mayor Sir William Walworth, a fishmonger, stabbed Wat Tyler at Smithfield in 1381. The hall isn't open to the public but if you peer through the railings on the left of the building (with the river behind you), you can see some of the finery displayed within.

The Fishmongers' Company is responsible for organising Britain's oldest annual sporting event: Doggett's Coat and Badge Race, contested by six Thames Watermen, has been held annually since 1715.

23. Fountain Court & Garden Court, EC4

Transport: Blackfriars tube/rail or Temple tube

The Inner and Middle Temple are two of the four surviving Inns of Court (along with Gray's Inn and Lincoln's Inn) and comprise a self-contained, ancient world of their own, tucked away between Fleet Street and the River Thames. This attractive, atmospheric enclave is the heart of legal London and full of picturesque corners, courts and thoroughfares. Despite this, its very existence is often unknown to the crowds who pass to the north and south of the Inns.

> Fountain Court has some important literary associations: this is where John Westlock met Ruth Finch in Charles Dickens's *Martin Chuzzlewit*.

Spacious and tranquil, Fountain Court has some venerable old trees, including an ancient mulberry, and is surrounded by striking buildings, notably Middle Temple Hall. There's been a fountain here since 1680-1, which was reputedly London's first permanent water feature. The sound of tinkling water adds to the almost rustic air of this unusually quiet part of central London.

Middle Temple Hall is Fountain Court's crowning glory, one of the finest surviving Elizabethan halls in Britain. The original hall dates from around 1320, although the one we see today was built in 1563-73. It has a glorious double hammer beam roof and was the site of the first performance of Shakespeare's *Twelfth Night* in 1602. A notable feature of Middle Temple Hall is the 29ft (9m) Bench Table, allegedly a gift from Elizabeth I and made from a single oak tree on her Windsor estate; the benchers who run the Middle Temple still dine off it. In front of the Bench is a small table traditionally known as the Cupboard, supposedly made of wood from the hatch of Sir Francis Drake's ship, *The Golden Hind*.

Down two short flights of steps from Fountain Court is Garden Court, which is next to Middle Temple Gardens (open weekdays, noon-3pm, May, June, July and September). There's not much to the small, plain court itself but it affords good views over the adjacent gardens – which is useful when they're closed – and of the attractive surrounding buildings.

Middle Temple Gardens are a peaceful haven running down to the road that flanks the north bank of the Thames here. They are most famous for their feature borders of red and white roses.

In Shakespeare's *Henry VI, Part I*, Middle Temple Gardens is where the red rose of Lancaster and the white rose of York were first plucked, by Richard Plantagenet and the Earl of Somerset, marking the beginning of the English War of the Roses (1455-85).

Middle Temple Hall exterior

Fountain Court

Middle Temple Hall

24. Fruiterers Passage, EC4

Transport: Cannon Street tube/rail

Fruiterers Passage, adjacent to Southwark Bridge on the north bank of the river, is a low-ceilinged underpass that runs under the bridge, now part of the Thames Path. It was built in the early '20s and is surprisingly attractive, with tiled designs on both sides. These show scenes of old London, including well-executed drawings and architects' plans of Southwark Bridge, in addition to panoramic views of other parts of the city, many dating from 1851. The tiles make Fruiterers Passage rather more inviting than the majority of London's underpasses and passages, many of which are dank, dark, malodorous and vaguely threatening.

Fruiterers Passage derives its name from the Worshipful Company of Fruiterers, whose origins date back to the 13th century (it's one of the oldest City Livery Companies) and which had a warehouse nearby. First mentioned in 1292 (as the Free Fruiterers), the company received ordinances in 1463 and a charter in 1606, granted by King James I. Despite such historical connections, Fruiterers Passage has only been known by this name for around a dozen years.

> The Fruiterers' function was to assess fruit entering the City and identify the duty payable on it.

Fruiterers' Coat of Arms

25. Garlick Hill, EC4

Transport: Mansion House tube

Garlick Hill is so-called because garlic was once landed and sold here. Today, it leads to a pretty church and an unusual statue. The church is St James Garlickhythe, which has pagan-like grapes around its gates (the Vintners' Hall is just across the road). Inside its curiosities include three ceiling panels painted with clouded blue sky, sword rests, an impressive organ case and a mummified body kept in a vestry cupboard.

> The mummy, known as Jimmy Garlick, once featured in the television series *Mummy Autopsy*, which concluded that he died between 1641 and 1801.

The statue outside the church is by Vivien Mallock and is called *The (Vintners' Company) Barge Master and Swan Marker*. It portrays the master wearing traditional costume with an attentive swan at his feet, and celebrates a curious ceremony known as Swan Upping which takes place annually in the third week of July.

The ritual involves swanherds making a five-day journey upstream to Abingdon, aboard traditional Thames skiffs, during which they count, weigh, measure and tag swans along the way, as well checking their general well-being. Swan Upping dates back to the 12th century when the Crown claimed ownership of all mute swans, a valuable source of food. The Crown maintains ownership to this day, which it shares with the Vintners' and Dyers' Livery Companies.

26. Gough Square, EC4

Transport: Blackfriars tube/rail

Gough Square is actually a long, irregular lane leading to a small, rectangular square. It's named for a family of wool merchants who owned it in the 18th century and is best known as the site of Dr Johnson's House. Samuel Johnson (1709-84) was a biographer, editor, essayist, lexicographer, literary critic, novelist and poet (and obviously a splendid time manager). He was also the subject of perhaps the world's most famous biography, by his friend James Boswell.

Gough Square boasts a small bronze statue of Hodge, one of Dr Johnson's cats, shown sitting next to a pair of empty oyster shells on top of a copy of the famous dictionary, with the inscription 'a very fine cat indeed'.

The square is in an atmospheric maze of courtyards and passages to the north of Fleet Street, where it's easy to imagine bumping into Dr Johnson himself. His house is an elegant Georgian building, where he lived from 1748-59 and completed the first comprehensive English dictionary. Grade I listed, it was built c.1700 and is one of the few houses of its period surviving in the City of London (there are plenty in other parts of the capital). It has been restored to its original condition and contains exhibits about Johnson's life and work.

27. Groveland Court, EC4

Transport: Mansion House tube

Groveland Court is opposite number 43 Bow Lane (see page 76). It's short, cosy and quaint, with a distinctly Dickensian atmosphere, and is the location of Williamson's Tavern which claims to hold the City's oldest excise licence. The building dates from the 17th century but the current bar is a pre-war rebuild.

Until 1735, the building was the Lord Mayor of London's official residence and one of the rooms is called Mansion House Lounge in acknowledgement of this. Later, Robert Williamson acquired the property and turned it into a hotel. The court was known as New Court in those days and only became Groveland Court quite recently.

It's claimed that the wrought iron gates (monogrammed with the letters WM) at the pub's entrance were a gift from William III, who dined here with Queen Mary as guests of the Lord Mayor. The pub is said to be equidistant from all the City's outer limits and is therefore right in the middle of the Square Mile, which is marked by a stone in the parlour. The fireplace in the smaller bar is built partly of Roman tiles which were excavated on the site.

Like many City pubs, Williamson's is only open Monday to Friday (11am-11pm) and closed at weekends.

Williamson's Tavern

28. Inner Temple Lane, EC4

Transport: Blackfriars tube/rail or Temple tube

The City's only surviving timber-framed Jacobean townhouse is on Fleet Street. It's known as Prince Henry's Room (see below) and under it a pair of aged wooden doors in a 12th-century stone doorway open into Inner Temple Lane. This, in turn, leads into one of central London's loveliest areas, the Inner and Middle Temple (see page 95) and the magnificent Temple Church.

The area's origins date back to the late 12th century, when the Knights Templar built a base here and established the Temple Church. Subsequently, the property passed to the Knights Hospitallers, who leased some of it to lawyers. Later still, it passed to the Crown and in 1609 James I granted the Temple to the Benchers (senior members or Masters) of the Inner and Middle Temple. The church is elegant and impressive, but much rebuilt and restored over the centuries.

> Temple Church has a starring role in Dan Brown's novel *The Da Vinci Code*.

Prince Henry's Room itself has had a varied history, including spells as a tavern and a waxworks. It's so-called because of a claim that James I's eldest son Prince Henry (1594-1612) used the building as a council chamber (albeit briefly, as he died at 18). It's a remarkable survivor and shows what London would have looked like before the Great Fire.

Prince Henry's Room

Temple Church

29. King's Bench Walk, EC4

Transport: Blackfriars tube/rail or Temple tube

Hidden away in the attractive, peaceful Inner Temple, King's Bench Walk is a wide and elegant thoroughfare that looks much as it would have done when Sir Christopher Wren built it in the late 17th century. Most of the buildings are red brick and date from 1677-8, although numbers 9-11 are – inexplicably and slightly jarringly – in yellow brick; they were built much later (1814), by Sir Robert Smirke.

The Walk has a long list of interesting former residents. Number 4 was the home of writers Sir Harold Nicolson and his wife Vita Sackville-West from 1930 to 1945. Author H. Rider Haggard lived at number 13 for a while, and novelist and poet George Moore lived at number 8 in 1888-96.

King's Bench Walk also houses the splendidly-named, Orwellian-sounding Alienation Office. Its business was the regulation of 'alienation', i.e. the unauthorised transfer of feudal lands without a government licence. Despite the date of 1577 emblazoned above the door, the first regulator of such procedures was established much earlier, during Henry III's reign (1216-72). Today the building houses barristers' chambers.

> During his early legal career, Tony Blair met his while Cherie while working in chambers at number 11 King's Bench Walk.

30. Laurence Pountney Hill, EC4

Transport: Monument tube

Short, quiet Laurence Pountney Hill packs in a fair amount of interest, both architectural and historical. Numbers 1 and 2 date from around 1703 and are two of the City's finest early 18th-century houses. They're designed to mirror each other as a pair and have elaborate, decorative wooden entrances, reached up a flight of steps.

At its southern end, the hill becomes wider, in two stages. A blue plaque marks the site of Corpus Christi College and Laurence Pountney Church (destroyed in 1666), which had been named after a local resident, Sir John de Pulteney, who was Lord Mayor four times in the 1330s.

Vestry House detail

At the bottom of the hill is the attractive Vestry House, parts of which date to the 14th century – it even boasts a section of Roman wall in the basement. However, much of the house is a rebuild from 1678, after the Great Fire, and it's now a Grade II listed private residence and the winner of a City Heritage Award.

In earlier times, the hill had the rather delightful name Green Lettuce Lane – or rather Grene Lattyce, in reference to a tavern with wooden lattice windows.

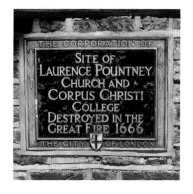

31. Leather Lane, EC1

Transport: Chancery Lane tube or Farringdon tube/rail

Leather Lane runs north off Holborn, initially along the east side of the impressive former Prudential Building at 138-142 Holborn, one of Victorian London's Gothic landmarks, now called Holborn Bars (but often still referred to as the Prudential Building).

> The original red-brick and terracotta Prudential Building was designed by Alfred Waterhouse and dates from 1879, with subsequent extensions that followed the original style. The Prudential sold the building in 1999 and it's now an events venue.

On the right of Leather Lane is a Nicholson's pub, the Sir Christopher Hatton (Elizabeth I's Chancellor, after whom nearby Hatton Garden is named), opposite which you can enter the Prudential Building's central courtyard and admire its internal façade. Further north, the lane becomes a slightly scruffy and vaguely bohemian market, selling clothes, food and general goods. There are plenty of places to eat, many offering Mediterranean and Asian cuisines.

Leather Lane is in stark contrast to the surrounding streets that sell gold and precious stones, most notably the abovementioned Hatton Garden, the heart of London's jewellery district. The lane was once, unsurprisingly, the preserve of leather traders, although its name is thought to come from an inn which once stood here, The Greyhound (*leveroun* in old French).

Holborn Bars

Leather Lane Market

32. Magpie Alley & Ashentree Court, EC4

Transport: Blackfriars tube/rail

Like many streets in the City, Magpie Alley gets its name from an old drinking den, although the 18th-century Magpie tavern which once stood in nearby Whitefriars Street is long gone. At the end of the alley is Ashentree Court, a treeless space with a small section of medieval crypt imaginatively encased in glass.

The crypt was part of the extensive Whitefriars Monastery, which originally stretched from Fleet Street down to the Thames, and from the Temple east to Water Lane (now Whitefriars Street). The friars were an order of Carmelites, thought to be named after Mt Carmel in the Holy Land (now northern Israel) where the order is believed to have been founded in the 12th century. They were based here from around 1240 until the monastery was dissolved in 1538 on the orders of Henry VIII.

Nothing of the monastery remains above ground but much was found during excavations in the late 19th century and the '20s, most notably this starkly attractive section of crypt. It was originally on the east side of the square but during an '80s redevelopment it was raised onto a concrete raft and moved to its present location.

Magpie Alley leads off Bouverie Street and is decorated with tiles showing images of printing, once an important industry in this part of London.

Whitefriars Crypt

33. Martin Lane, EC4

Transport: Monument tube or Cannon Street tube/rail

Martin Lane is named after the church of St Martin Orgar, which was demolished in the early 19th century. First mentioned in the 12th century, the church was destroyed in the Great Fire. French Protestants restored part of it and used it for worship for 150 years before it was demolished in 1820.

The church site is marked by a striking Italianate tower designed as a rectory for St Clement's Eastcheap in 1851-52 by John Davies, and currently used as offices. A blue plaque also marks the church's location and a small garden sits next to the tower.

Martin Lane is also the site of one of London's more historic drinking dens, the unusually named Olde Wine Shades. It's now an El Vino establishment but apparently has a history going back to 1663, which is the date stamped on a lead cistern found on the premises; as such it claims to be the oldest 'wine bar' in the City. It's an atmospheric place, with a Dickensian ambience and an attractive early Victorian frontage.

> The Shades was a common name for taverns in the 18th and 19th centuries, as they were often underground or shaded from the sun by an arcade or awning.

34. Panyer Alley, EC4

Transport: St Paul's tube

Best described as 'lost in plain sight', Panyer Alley is situated by the entrance to St Paul's tube station on Newgate Street. It used to be a narrow alley – possibly 15th century – but is now a wider passageway. Its main attraction can be spotted on the wall of Caffe Nero: a bas-relief of a naked boy astride a panyer, i.e. a bread basket (from the French *pannier*). Manufacturers of panyers were once based here to supply the bakers in nearby Bread Street.

> The jury is out on exactly what the panyer boy signifies. It might simply have been a sign for the tavern or to commemorate the boys who sold bread here. Or it might mark the site of an early medieval corn market or even have a pagan meaning, e.g. an emblem of plenty.

It's thought that the image was once on an outside wall of the Panyer Tavern which was around the corner on Paternoster Row, until being destroyed in 1666. Below is an inscription – 'When ye have sought, The Citty Round, Yet still this is, The Highest Ground' – with a date beneath, August the 27th

1688. But the inscription's claim is incorrect, as Cornhill is the City's highest spot, being around a foot higher than here. And it's thought that the bas-relief might predate the inscription under it; it certainly looks more weathered.

35. Peter's Lane, EC1

Transport: Farringdon tube/rail

Peter's Lane leads off Cowcross Street in an attractive part of lively Clerkenwell. The lane is pedestrian-only, less hectic than nearby streets, and runs along the side of the so-called Rookery (see below). Cowcross Street is a well-kept, upmarket thoroughfare, named for the place where cattle crossed the River Fleet on their way to Smithfield Market until it ceased trading in live animals in 1855.

> Clerkenwell itself is named after the Clerk's Well in Farringdon Lane, where the clerks of medieval London gathered to perform mystery plays.

The Rookery building on the corner of Cowcross Street and Peter's Lane dates from 1764. It used to be a slum and is now a chic boutique hotel occupying a trio of 18th-century buildings, cleverly and sensitively restored to retain many original features. Five handsome cow's head friezes run up the side of the building on Peter's Lane.

The term 'rookery' was a nickname for the overcrowded slums where the poor lived in the 18th and 19th centuries, alongside thieves, prostitutes and other undesirable individuals. The name may come from the haphazard, multi-storey design of the buildings, where people lived literally on top of one another, like rooks nesting in a tree.

Rookery Hotel

36. Queenhithe, EC4

Transport: Mansion House tube

Just to the west of Fruiterers Passage (see page 97), Queenhithe is an unassuming lane next to a square inlet on the north bank of the Thames. And yet this part of the riverbank is steeped in history as a sign on the river wall testifies. This is the Alfred Plaque, which was installed in 1986 to mark the 1,100th anniversary of King Alfred's resettlement of the Roman City of London in 886 – then called Lundenburgh.

> ## THE ALFRED PLAQUE
>
> This plaque was erected in 1986 to mark the eleven hundredth anniversary of King Alfred's resettlement of the Roman city of London in 886, after the abandonment of the Saxon town which had existed for some three centuries in the Strand area to the west of the City. At this place a harbour and market were established by 899 to restore trade after the Viking invasions.
>
> Erected by the Museum of London and Wates City of London Properties and unveiled by The Rt. Hon., The Lord Mayor, Sir David Rowe-Ham. G.B.E., on 25th November. 1986.

It's hard to imagine, but this unremarkable, slightly scruffy inlet was once the base for a thriving Saxon and medieval dockyard and trading post – and was one of the most important places in Saxon Lundenburgh. It was established in 899 during the reign of Ethelred II and for the first 100 years of its existence it was called Ethelreds-hythe (Ethelred's port).

The name changed when Henry I took the throne and renamed it in honour of his Queen Matilda. Queenhithe, as it became known, is the City's oldest dock and was the last to be demolished, with some of its buildings surviving into the late 20th century.

> An older Saxon town called Lundenwic had existed from the early 7th century in the area around the Strand and Aldwych, but had been abandoned due to Viking invasions.

37. Quiet Garden to Cardinal Basil Hume, Lamb's Passage, EC1

Transport: Barbican or Old Street tube

In the northwest of the City is a small but delightful green corner dedicated to one of Britain's most popular religious leaders. A plaque on wall states 'this quiet garden is dedicated to the memory of Basil Hume, monk and shepherd, 1923-1999.' Opened in 2003 – it was previously the car park of St Joseph's Church – it was created by Father Bruno Healy and landscape gardener Simon Peter Stobart.

> Basil Hume was Archbishop of Westminster and later a Cardinal of the Roman Catholic church, popular with Catholics and non-Catholics for his warm and humble demeanour.

The garden is between Old Street and Barbican tube stations, on Lamb's Passage, which is close to the old Bunhill Fields cemetery. (The name Bunhill might come from Bone Hill, a reference to the area's long use for burials.) It's small – a mere 30ft by 30ft – and overshadowed by office blocks, but there's plenty packed into this tiny space, including a variety of planting and trees, benches, a stream and wind chimes; creepers crawl over the railings and bamboo fronds help to give it the air of an oasis.

The Cardinal would surely approve, as he would its purpose: to spread the church's influence into the neighbourhood to reach people who would otherwise have little contact with it.

Cardinal Hume

38. Salters' Hall Court, EC4

Transport: Cannon Street tube/rail

Salters' Hall Court is opposite the recently-refurbished Cannon Street Station and alongside the impressive, gleaming-metallic Walbrook Building, one of the City's newer landmarks. The court leads to the peaceful, unexpected St Swithun's Church garden, which lies to the rear of the Walbrook Building.

> Salters' Hall Court was also the home of London's first Lord Mayor, Henry Fitz-Ailwyn, who held office from 1189 to 1212.

The small garden is located on the former churchyard of St Swithin London Stone, first founded in the 13th century, and is thought to be the burial site of Catrin Glyndwr, daughter of Welsh leader Owain Glyndwr, who died in 1413 after being imprisoned in the Tower of London. This is perhaps why the garden's oddly designed modern sculpture has an inscription in Welsh and English. The garden also has the gravestone of a Nathaniel Thornton (died 1839) and some benches, providing a small haven from which to admire the Walbrook Building's curves.

The court is named after the Worshipful Company of Salters, which once had its base in St Swithin's Lane (its hall is now in Fore Street). Salt was a vital commodity in medieval England, particularly for the preservation of fish and meat, making the Salters an important guild.

Salters' Coat of Arms

39. Stationers' Hall Court, EC4

Transport: St Paul's tube

Stationers' Hall Court is a narrow, unassuming passageway that leads off Ludgate Hill. It's easy to overlook, but is worth investigating as it opens out into a spacious courtyard that houses the Stationers' Hall.

The north-eastern end of Stationers' Hall Court leads into Ave Maria Lane, named after the prayers said by the medieval clergy of nearby St Paul's Cathedral as they processed around the local area.

The Stationers' Company dates from 1403; it received its Royal Charter in 1557 and was initially based closer to St Paul's Cathedral. Its first dedicated hall on this site was built in 1606 and destroyed in the Great Fire 60 years later. The building we see today is Grade I listed and is the company's fourth, built in 1673. It was refronted in 1800 and the Portland stone east wing dates from 1885-7. An impressive array of mounted heraldic shields can be seen through the hall's windows, although it isn't open to visitors.

The Stationers' Hall luckily escaped serious damage during the Second World War and has become a popular venue for functions and marriages, tucked away in this centrally-located enclave.

40. Took's Court, EC4

Transport: Chancery Lane tube

Took's Court is situated off Furnival Street and is one of the myriad alleys, courts and lanes that once meandered through the area between Chancery Lane and Fetter Lane, most of which no longer exist. The L-shaped court is probably named after a Thomas Tooke, who built it in around 1650 and constructed a number of tenements here and on land to the north.

> This area wasn't always so salubrious. In 1814 the writer and sometime MP Richard Brinsley Sheridan was incarcerated in a debtors' prison in Took's Court.

Numbers 14-16 are stylish 18th-century terraced houses and are listed buildings. Charles Dickens once lived at number 15 and a sign outside it says 'Dickens House'. Like many buildings in the area it now houses legal professionals. The prominent civil liberties law firm Tooks Chambers was located in Took's Court until 2013, but was dissolved following cuts to legal aid funding.

The court is also the site of an interesting piece of wartime construction, which was ordered by Winston Churchill in the '40s. It's an underground shelter, one of eight built in London, designed to accommodate around 8,000 key personnel in safety, partly against attack by V2 rockets. It's located 100 feet below Took's Court, with an anonymous entrance on High Holborn.

41. Wardrobe Place, EC4

Transport: Blackfriars tube/rail or St Paul's tube

Initially a low-ceilinged, short passageway off Carter Lane (see page 79), Wardrobe Place widens out into an attractive, peaceful courtyard. It's an example of the type of residential courtyard that was once common in the City: quiet, understated and with a few trees to provide shade and refresh the air, it's a pleasant and central place to live. Today, some of it remains little altered since being rebuilt after the Great Fire – numbers 3-5 date from around 1720 – but parts of the courtyard were redeveloped in the '80s.

Wardrobe Place is said to be haunted by the ghost of a lady who's seen dressed in white and drifting from door to door shortly after dusk.

Wardrobe Place is most famous for being the site of the King's Wardrobe, as shown by a blue plaque. This 'wardrobe' was actually a large house used by Edward III to store his ceremonial robes and various other possessions. He acquired the property in 1359 from Sir John Beauchamp and the monarch moved his wardrobe here from its previous home in the Tower of London. Sadly, the Wardrobe burnt down in 1666.

42. Wine Office Court, EC4

Transport: Chancery Lane or Temple tube

Wine Office Court is a narrow, covered passage off Fleet Street that leads to a historic pub, Ye Olde Cheshire Cheese. The court's name sounds like a reference to wine sold at the hostelry, but actually comes from the licences for selling wine which were issued at the excise office on this spot.

The pub's name comes either from the cheese that ousted Suffolk as London's most popular at the time or a 16th-century landlord, Thomas Cheshire.

The pub was the first building to be rebuilt in 1667 after the Great Fire, although it was already a century and a half old when the flames destroyed it. Its vaulted cellar is even older, thought to have belonged to a 13th-century Carmelite monastery which once occupied the site. The pub is little changed since the 17th century and a sign outside lists the 15 monarchs who have reigned throughout its existence; another sign details its famous patrons.

These allegedly included Dr Johnson (a local resident – see Gough Square on page 99), Sir Joshua Reynolds, Edward Gibbon, Charles Dickens, David Garrick, Thomas Carlyle, Alfred Lord Tennyson, W. M. Thackeray, Mark Twain, Theodore Roosevelt, Arthur Conan Doyle, G. K. Chesterton and W. B. Yeats. The pub is an attractive, creaky warren of bars, especially atmospheric in winter when a fire is burning.

Barbican ⊖

BEECH STREET

ALDERSGATE ST

Barbican Centre

4

Museum of London

Moorgate ⊖

MOORGATE

CHISWELL ST

ELDON ST

Liverpool Street Station

Liverpool Street ⊖

15

Old Spitalfields Market

26

16

1

BISHOPGATE

31

7

9

27

LONDON WALL

5

LONDON WALL

14

33

HOUNDSDITCH

12

MOORGATE

20

GRESHAM

24

Guildhall

21

STREET

2

19

29

22

LOTHBURY

LEADENHALL

STREET

Aldgate ⊖

CHEAPSIDE

17

Bank ⊖

POULTRY

Bank of England

THREADNEEDLE ST

Royal Exchange

CORNHILL

Lloyds

STREET

QUEEN VICTORIA STREET

Mansion House

10

6

3

8

FENCHURCH

13

18

Fenchurch Street Station

CANNON

STREET

KING WILLIAM ST

LOMBARD STREET

GRACECHURCH ST

30

32

11

Tower Hill ⊖

Cannon Street ⊖

Cannon Street Station

Monument ⊖

EASTCHEAP

23

GREAT TOWER ST

25

28

34

TOWER HILL

Southwark Bridge

London Bridge

LOWER THAMES STREET

Tower of London

St Katharine Docks

RIVER   THAMES

Tower Bridge

CHAPTER 3

CITY EAST & EAST LONDON

1. Artillery Lane, E1

Transport: Liverpool Street tube/rail

Artillery Lane leads off pedestrian-thronged Bishopsgate near Liverpool Street station. Built in the late 1600s, it was previously called Artillery Yard and, like many of the streets around here, it has a strong link with weaponry. This area, on the edge of London's vibrant financial district, was, in the later Middle Ages, a battlefield of a different sort: a training ground for the Honourable Artillery Company. Gunners practised here from the mid-1500s until 1682.

> The Honourable Artillery Company dates back to the 11th century and is the second-oldest military organisation in the world.

Honourable Artillery Company

Artillery Lane now hosts a mixture of businesses, restaurants and bars, including the civilised Williams Ale & Cider House. The upper levels of the building opposite this bar are an example of the successful restoration of a former warehouse. Further along the lane, on the corner with Gun Street is another type of architectural rescue, this one an example of 'facadism'. This is the practice of leaving a historic façade in place when the building behind is knocked down. If done well, the contrast between the old façade and new structure behind it can look vibrant and interesting. But if done clumsily, it can appear odd, if not downright silly. The historic façade that remains here is controversial, as it's slightly adrift of the new building, with large metal pins holding it at arm's length. Worse, its blank, empty windows are out of kilter with those behind.

By way of contrast, numbers 56 and 58 Artillery Lane are an architectural success story and a very welcome survival from the Georgian era. They're 'paired houses' –adjoining properties – and their elegant, historical frontages appear to be from a Jane Austin film set. But they're actually original, built in the early 18th century and remodelled in 1756-7.

Williams Ale & Cider House

These elegant Georgian 'paired houses' were originally occupied by two prosperous Huguenot silk merchants, Nicholas Jourdain and Francis Rybot.

Number 56 is of particular note, generally regarded as London's finest surviving mid-Georgian shop front, with varied, interesting detail that deserves close inspection. It's Grade I listed, while number 58 is the relatively poor relation, with an early 19th-century, plain Regency frontage and only Grade II listed.

56 Artillery Lane

2. Austin Friars, EC2

Transport: Bank tube or Liverpool Street tube/rail

Historical, meandering Austin Friars has a covered entrance on Old Broad Street and is informally divided into three sections. Sections of the street have standard lamps, stone flagstones and Victorian buildings, which add character and interest. The name Austin Friars comes from the important Augustinian monastery founded here in 1253. The monastery's boundaries were Copthall Avenue, London Wall and Throgmorton Street, and it was dissolved on the orders of Henry VIII in the 16th century.

Its chapel managed to survive, however, and was eventually given to London's population of expatriate Danes, Dutch and Germans, becoming known as the Dutch Church. The church building we see today – at 7 Austin Friars – dates only from 1957, the old one having been destroyed in the Blitz after managing to survive the Great Fire of 1666. It's built to an unusual design, with a distinctive style and shape.

Number 12 Austin Friars is Furniture Makers' Hall, while at number 29 is the small rear entrance of the Drapers' Hall, once home to Thomas Cromwell (see Throgmorton Avenue on page 156 for more about this).

Stained glass, Dutch Church

Established in 1963, the Furniture Makers are one of the City's newest Livery Companies, with their first Hall, in Austin Friars, dating from 2005.

3. Ball Court, EC3

Transport: Bank tube

The area around Birchin Lane, Cornhill and Lombard Street has a series of attractive alleys, courts and passageways. Many are narrow, winding and redolent of older times, and quite a contrast with the contemporary City of the Gherkin, Lloyd's of London and other modern monoliths.

Ball Court and its surrounds feel more Dickensian than 21st century. But the Court is actually older – 18th century – a tiny, narrow, partly-covered passage off the north side of Cornhill. It opens into a modest courtyard outside bow-windowed Simpson's Tavern (open Monday for lunch, Tuesday to Friday for breakfast and lunch). Tables made from wine barrels dot the court, which is often crowded with customers enjoying pre-lunch drinks.

Originally founded in 1723 on Bell Lane in Billingsgate, Simpson's has been here since 1757. It's a (rare) survivor of a once-common institution – the London chophouse – and was initially a wine and spirit merchant, becoming a 'restaurant' in 1808. Today it's noted for its traditional English food and atmospheric interior, with warm, dark wood panelling. Beyond Simpson's, Ball Court leads into Castle Court and thence to St Michael's Alley and Bengal Court, site of the George & Vulture, another City dining institution (see page 124).

Charles Dickens was a regular at Simpson's Tavern, where women weren't admitted until 1916.

Simpson's

4. The Barbican, EC2

Transport: Barbican tube or Moorgate tube/rail

The vast, concrete Barbican development has surprisingly ancient roots. The name Barbican comes from a defensive fortification, probably a watchtower. There must have been many such towers along the adjacent City wall which ran past here from Roman through to medieval times; impressive traces remain nearby.

The area was extensively damaged during the Blitz and it was decided to build a residential complex. This was completed in 1973, while the adjacent Barbican Centre for Arts and Conferences was finished in 1982. The whole development covers around 40 acres (15.2 hectares) and includes 2,014 flats in blocks and towers. They're of aggregate concrete, built around courts or plazas, joined by elevated walkways. The primary design influence was Le Corbusier and the development is Grade II listed.

The Barbican's Conservatory is open on selected days once or twice a week from 11am to 5.30pm (noon-5.30pm on bank holidays). Open days are posted on the website around a month in advance.

There are some tranquil areas tucked away amidst all the concrete. The Lakeside Terrace comprises a central public court and café, with space to stroll by a large expanse of water. The complex also boasts a Conservatory, London's second-largest, which has more than 2,000 species of tropical plants and trees, as well as finches, quails and exotic fish.

5. Basinghall Avenue, EC2

Transport: Moorgate tube/rail

Basinghall Avenue lies off the north end of Coleman Street. It's the site of the intriguingly-named Girdlers' Hall (right), with its smart, modestly-sized garden. The latter is an unexpected and welcome patch of green in the heart of the City of London, with benches around a small lawn, low box hedging and young trees, including a mulberry tree descended from an arboreal ancestor from 1750.

> The Girdlers' Hall garden regularly wins prizes in City of London garden competitions (and there are more gardens in the City than might be expected).

The Avenue is named after the influential Basing family who had a house here in the 13th century. The Girdlers' Company – makers of belts and girdles – dates from at least the early 14th century and gained a royal charter in 1449. The Hall is located on a site that they've owned since 1431.

The Girdlers haven't had much luck with their halls. The first (1431) was destroyed in the Great Fire of 1666 and the subsequent one flattened during the Blitz of the Second World War. The current building is attractive, elegant and in period style, designed by C. Ripley and built in 1960-61.

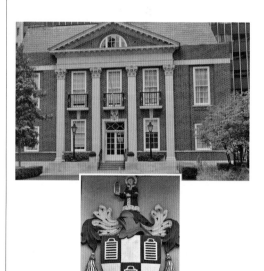

Girdlers' Coat of Arms

6. Bengal Court, Castle Court & St Michael's Alley, EC3

Transport: Bank tube

Bengal Court leads off Birchin Lane (opposite Cowper's Court); the entrance is no wider than a doorway, so it's easy to miss. Dating back at least 300 years, it's one of a series of atmospheric, historic passageways that wind around Cornhill. On the left at the end of Bengal Court is the side of the famous George & Vulture (see

opposite), one of the City's (rare) surviving chophouses (see also Ball Court and Simpson's on page 121).

One of the George & Vulture's entrances is on St Michael's Alley, which leads off at a right angle from Bengal Court. The alley is also home to the Jamaica Wine House (above); thus it has the distinction of hosting two of London's oldest and most distinguished places of refreshment.

The current premises occupies an attractive, redbrick building built in 1869, with a large, distinctive sign in the style of an old lamp. Inside, there are high ceilings, a wood-panelled bar and plenty of original Victorian

The Jamaica Wine House (above right) – or The Jampot as it's sometimes known locally – is on the site of what's thought to be London's first coffee house, dating from 1652 (shown by a plaque). Samuel Pepys was an early patron, visiting in 1660.

features. The Jamaica Inn (Mon-Fri, 11am-11pm – closed at weekends) is currently owned by the Kent brewery Shepherd Neame.

Leading off St Michael's Alley and parallel to Bengal Court is Castle Court, where there's the main entrance to the above-mentioned George & Vulture (open for lunch, Mon-Fri); note the attractive tiles around one of the large windows. There's been an inn on the site since 1268; the George & Vulture was established in 1600, although the current premises date from 1748. The Dickensian atmosphere of both the venue and the surrounding area is authenticated by the fact that the chophouse is mentioned a

> Walk to the Cornhill end of St Michael's Alley for a peek at St Michael-in-Cornhill (below). This attractive City church has a list of rectors dating back to 1133 and an interesting exterior, although the interior is perhaps rather over-restored.

number of times in *The Pickwick Papers*. The author himself was a regular here and it's claimed to have been a meeting place for the notorious libertines who formed The Hellfire Club. If that's not enough infamy for you, the ghost of a grey lady is said to haunt the upstairs dining room.

7. Brune Street & Tenter Ground, E1

Transport: Aldgate East tube or Liverpool Street tube/rail

A turning off White's Row, Tenter Ground is a short street with a strikingly handsome Huguenot building on the right. It was possibly a weavers' workshop as the area was once a centre for weaving; the name Tenter Ground comes from the tenters (wooden frames) on which woven cloth was stretched to help it dry evenly. Turn left into Brune Street to see another interesting building: the eye-catching Soup Kitchen for the Jewish Poor.

Soup kitchens were once commonplace in the deprived East End, but it's rare to find one as attractive and ornate as this. The design was deliberate. Many of the Jewish immigrants to East London in the later 19th century struggled and in 1902 the Jewish community built this soup kitchen to help them.

Its impressive facade testifies to the wealth of some of the area's Jewish traders and was intended to show their less fortunate brothers that with hard work and drive they could also succeed. The building was also designed to persuade existing residents that Jewish immigrants weren't going to be a drain on public funds.

The soup kitchen has been converted into upmarket flats, but its lovely sandstone facade remains. Note the old 'Way In' and 'Way Out' signs above the doors.

8. Bull's Head Passage, EC3

Transport: Bank tube

Bull's Head Passage is opposite The Crosse Keys pub at 9 Gracechurch Street. It leads into the lovely Leadenhall Market, an ornate, covered Victorian market of wrought iron and glass on the site of 1st-century London's Roman basilica. It isn't the market's most attractive passageway but it leads to many that are, most of them unnamed.

As for the name, there was a butcher's shop on or near the passage in the 17th century, while in the 18th century an inn (the Bull's Head Tavern) took over the site. In the 17th century it was usual to advertise a business by displaying an example of what it sold outside, in this case a bull's (or cow's) head; either a real one or a sign depicting one.

Bull's Head Passage is a narrow annexe to the market rather than an integral part of it and for many people the main reason for seeking it out is its Harry Potter film connection. In *Harry Potter and the Goblet of Fire*, the entrance to the wizards' inn The Leaky Cauldron was filmed here, at number 42 (actually an opticians).

Parts of Leadenhall Market (below) stand in for the magical high street Diagon Alley in some Harry Potter films.

9. Catherine Wheel Alley, E1

Transport: Liverpool Street tube/rail

Leading off Bishopsgate, the slim, arched entrance to Catherine Wheel Alley is easy to miss, squashed between a branch of Pret A Manger and the serviced apartments at number 196. It's paved and covered for a while before opening to the elements, and is a convenient cut-through to Middlesex Street and an escape from the crowds thronging Bishopsgate.

Narrow and claustrophobic, Catherine Wheel Alley's atmosphere is redolent of the old City. Tall, brown-brick buildings line it, although there's nothing of note. It doglegs left, then right, where it widens to accommodate vehicles (just). The intriguingly-named Cock Hill Road leads off to the right, running into New Street.

The alley is old, its name coming from a galleried coaching inn, The Catherine Wheel, which once stood at the Bishopsgate end. The first reference to it is in 1708 and it's said to have been one of Dick Turpin's meeting places in the early 18th century. It was damaged by fire in 1895 and demolished in 1911.

> Puritans objected to the name Catherine Wheel because it refers to the 9th-century saint and Catholic martyr St Catherine of Alexandria, and it was periodically changed to the neutral Cat and Wheel.

10. Change Alley, EC3

Transport: Bank tube

Change Alley has a number of entries and exits, notably onto Lombard Street and Cornhill. The exit to the latter is opposite the Royal Exchange, from which the alley derives its name (it was originally called Exchange Alley). It was once noted for its coffee houses, in particular Jonathan's and Garraway's; the site of the latter is marked by a carved sign featuring a grasshopper, part of the Gresham family crest. (It was Thomas Gresham who founded the Royal Exchange.)

Jonathan's was established around 1680 and is famous for being the meeting place of the speculators involved in the South Sea Bubble financial disaster. Later, it became a

Change Alley was also the site of the King's Arms Tavern, where the first meeting of the Marine Society was held in 1756.

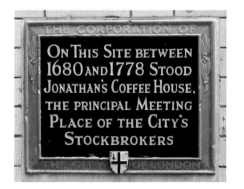

ON THIS SITE BETWEEN 1680 AND 1778 STOOD JONATHAN'S COFFEE HOUSE, THE PRINCIPAL MEETING PLACE OF THE CITY'S STOCKBROKERS

forerunner of the Stock Exchange, which subsequently moved to Threadneedle Street. Garraway's dates from 1669 and acted as a sort of auction house, with an association with the Hudson's Bay Company. Many items were traded here – including coffee, sugar and spice, furs and textiles, and the spoils of war – until its closure in 1872 (it's mentioned several times by Charles Dickens).

The buildings along the alley today are bland and modern (a number are banks) but Change Alley's rambling, higgledy-piggledy route still manages to be more reminiscent of the old City than the new.

11. Cooper's Row, EC3

Transport: Tower Hill tube

The area around Tower Hill underground station and off Trinity Square is an extension of Cooper's Row. Its most striking feature is a tall, eye-catching section of Roman and medieval wall, a remnant of the one that protected Roman Londinium. The wall was built in around 200AD from Kentish ragstone and ran in a two-mile arc from Tower Hill to Blackfriars, enclosing an area of 330 acres (134ha).

The section of wall here is around 100ft long and 35ft high. The lower half (up to about 15.5ft) is Roman, above that it's medieval. It's noteworthy that the Roman section is better constructed than the medieval part and includes layers of red tiles to strengthen it.

At 43 Trinity Square (see page 157), off Cooper's Row, is The Wine Library (open Monday, 10am-6pm, Tuesday to Friday, 10am-8pm), reached by a challenging spiral staircase. This plain, atmospheric cellar is a combination of wine bar, shop and restaurant (for a cheese and paté lunch). You can choose from around 400 wines and enjoy them at retail prices plus a modest corkage fee.

In front of the wall stands a life-sized, 19th-century statue of Trajan (left), Emperor 98-117AD. Tower Gardens, just behind the wall, provides an excellent vantage point from which to view it, with the nearby Tower of London and the distant Shard rearing up in the background.

12. Devonshire Row & Square, EC2

Transport: Liverpool Street tube/rail

Devonshire Row runs off Bishopsgate near Liverpool Street Station and leads to Devonshire Square. The row is narrow, low-rise and quite atmospheric, more tranquil than frantic Bishopsgate, but there's not much to detain you. Small, covered Cavendish Court leads off it, more Dickensian than modern.

Impressive Devonshire Square is at the end of the row, with Coopers Hall at number 13 and Osborne House next door at number 12. The skyscraping Heron Tower (right), officially 110 Bishopsgate, looms over the square, which was the site of the so-called Fisher's Folly, a 16th-century mansion built by a cash-strapped goldsmith, Jasper Fisher. He was eventually forced to sell the property and it was purchased by the Duke of Devonshire, who owned it from 1620-75, hence the name of the square and row. The mansion was subsequently sold to the speculative builder Nicholas Barbon, who knocked it down.

> Barbon's full name was Nicholas If-Jesus-Christ-Had-Not-Died-For-Thee-Thou-Hadst-Been-Damned Barebone, a 'gift' from his Puritan father.

A few Georgian houses remain in Devonshire Square and help it to retain a sense of history. It's most noted today for the cleverly converted warehouses both here and in adjacent Cutler's Gardens. They were built 1770-1820 for the East India Company, converted in 1978-82 and now house offices, bars and restaurants. It's worth taking the time to wander around this impressive development.

13. Fen Court, EC3

Transport: Fenchurch Street tube/rail

Fen Court, which links Fenchurch Street with Fenchurch Avenue, is best known as the site of the granite sculpture *Gilt of Cain*, an artistic collaboration between the sculptor Michael Visocchi and the poet Lemn Sissay. It commemorates the 2007 bicentenary of the abolition of the transatlantic slave trade and comprises 17 cylindrical columns surrounding a podium, the latter recalling an ecclesiastical pulpit or slave auctioneer's podium.

The columns suggest either stylised stems of sugar cane or a crowd gathered to hear a speaker or a group of slaves standing before an auctioneer's stance. Extracts from Sissay's specially commissioned poem are engraved into the granite, blending the language of the Stock Exchange with Biblical references.

Fen Court may take its name from the modern meaning of fen – a low-lying area of marshy ground – perhaps the result of a stream that once rose in nearby Fenchurch Street. Or it could come from *fenum*, i.e. hay, which was once sold here.

Fen Court is an apt site for this work, being in the Parish of St Edmund the King and St Mary Woolnoth, which has a strong connection with the abolitionist movement: St Mary Woolnoth's rector from 1780-1807 was Reverend John Newton, a former slave trader who became a preacher and worked with the leading abolitionist William Wilberforce.

14. Finsbury Circus, EC2

Transport: Moorgate tube/rail

Finsbury Circus is an elegant, elliptical space with a central garden, a haven of relative tranquillity in the north of the City of London. The circus covers 2.2 hectares and the name refers to its shape, which is similar to that of an ancient Roman circus. It was laid out in 1815-17 and its original elegant houses were built by William Montague, designed by the memorably-named George Dance the Younger.

The original houses are gone and the circus's properties were rebuilt in the mid-19th and early 20th centuries, a mixture of the impressive and the bland. Britannic House, built 1924-7 by Sir Edwin Lutyens and Grade II listed, has been described as the circus's crowning glory. As you walk around Finsbury Circus, you notice that the layout and atmosphere are rather different from much of the City, reminiscent of an upmarket residential area in the West End.

Since 2010, Finsbury Circus has been a main worksite for the Crossrail development, so some garden features have been replaced by plant and machinery until at least 2016.

Britannic House

The central garden has a fine assortment of trees, including 200-year-old plane trees and a Japanese pagoda tree. It has also had a bowling green since 1925 and a bandstand since 1955.

15. Folgate Street & Elder Street, E1

Transport: Liverpool Street tube/rail

Leading off where Norton Folgate meets Shoreditch High Street, Folgate Street is a highlight of Huguenot East London (also see Fournier Street opposite). It happily retains the attractive, well-preserved terraces of 18th-century houses, and number 18 – Dennis Severs' House (right) – has been turned into an interactive museum, one of London's more unusual and imaginative attractions.

Folgate Street has a civilised pub, The Water Poet, which is on the corner with Blossom Street. Real ales and good food are on offer.

Severs was an American artist who filled his house with period fittings and furniture, so that each of the ten rooms reflects a different era of the house's history. It's now a sort of 'performance art' museum, designed to create an atmosphere redolent of the past and paint a picture of what life was like, including appropriate sounds and smells. Tours take around 45 minutes and cost from £7 (tel. 020-7247 4013 for details and to book).

Elder Street, leading off Folgate Street, dates from the 1730s and has more attractive Huguenot architecture and arguably an even more authentic feel. Number 32 has a blue plaque to painter Mark Gertler (1891-1939), who was born in nearby Gun Street.

16. Fournier Street & Surrounds, E1

Transport: Aldgate East tube or Liverpool Street tube/rail

Fournier Street leads off Commercial Street, with elegant Christ Church Spitalfields (right) on one side, the Ten Bells pub on the other – two of the East End's most famous locations. The church is by Nicholas Hawksmoor, a pupil of Sir Christopher Wren. Built in 1714, it originally served the area's Huguenot community; over half of the 18th-century gravestones bear French names.

The Grade II listed Ten Bells (below) dates from 1755. During the Victorian era, prostitutes picked up clients here and two of Jack the Ripper's victims – Annie Chapman and Mary Kelly – visited the pub just before their murders.

> Mary Kelly was the Ripper's final victim in November 1888, whose mutilated body was discovered in Miller's Court, not far from the Ten Bells (below).

Fournier Street is a fine 18th-century thoroughfare, lined with rows of tall, attractive buildings which originally housed Huguenot silk merchants, master weavers and retailers. Numbers 17-25 retain attic windows which were added to maximise the light inside for the weavers who worked here before the street became residential. Number 23 was built 1726-8 for the minister of the church and is a rare example of a Hawksmoor residential building, while numbers 10 and 12

have been the home and workplace of artists Gilbert and George since the '60s. There's also a touch of Harry Potter here, with a number 'Eleven and a Half' Fournier Street.

Fire insurance marks were often made from copper or lead and are very collectable (many have been stolen).

Number 7 has a plaque embossed with the crest of an insurance company. These were once common on buildings, in the days before a 'proper' fire service, when individual insurance companies often had their own fire fighting crews. They only extinguished fires in buildings insured by the relevant insurance company (identified by the badges) or, for a fee, fires in buildings insured by other companies.

Wilkes Street leads off Fournier Street and Princelet Street runs off that. Both are worth investigating for their attractive, Huguenot-era buildings. At the junction of Fournier Street and Brick Lane is the Brick Lane Jamme Masjid (Great Mosque), the

Sun dial on Jamme Masjid

only building in the world outside Israel to have been a church, synagogue and mosque. Georgian in style and Grade II* listed, it was built in 1743 as a Protestant chapel by Huguenots and later became a Wesleyan chapel, then a Methodist one. In the late 19th century, it was converted into the Machzike Adass Great Synagogue to serve Jewish refugees from Eastern Europe. The '70s saw an influx of Bangladeshi immigrants and in 1976 the building was refurbished and became a mosque.

Fournier Street

17. Frederick's Place, EC2

Transport: Bank tube

This attractive, charming cul-de-sac leads off Old Jewry and is an unexpected corner of calm in the hectic City. Frederick's Place stands out from the surrounding area, much of which comprises high-rise, modern buildings, because it's lined with distinguished, 18th-century terraced houses (many are Grade II listed). They give the street a residential feel, although today most are offices.

> The noted architectural critic Nicolas Pevsner described Frederick's Place as 'an oasis of domesticity'.

The houses were built by the famous Adam brothers in 1776 on a site where Sir John Frederick (Lord Mayor of London in 1661) had owned a property. Number 1 has a blue plaque to the eminent accountant Edwin Waterhouse (1841-1917, of PricewaterhouseCoopers fame) who worked here from 1899-1905.

Number 6 displays a blue plaque to mark the fact that Benjamin Disraeli (1804-81, Prime Minister in 1868 and 1874-80) was articled to a firm of solicitors here in 1821-24. It was at this time that he began to behave and dress in a notably flamboyant way, and also to contemplate a life beyond a legal existence in tranquil, understated Frederick's Place.

18. French Ordinary Court, EC3

Transport: Fenchurch Street tube/rail

The arched, covered entrance to French Ordinary Court leads off Crutched Friars (next to the Lloyd's Club) and promises more than it delivers. For the court – which leads under Fenchurch Street Station and on to St Katherine's Row – is dimly lit and slightly sinister.

There's little to see, the interest being in the atmosphere and the origin of the name. An 'ordinary' was a type of eating house, quite common in the City of London during the 17th and 18th centuries. Ordinaries specialised in inexpensive, fixed-price meals and were the bistros of their day. One was established here in the later 17th century, either by or in order to cater to local French expatriates.

The noted diarist, MP and naval administrator Samuel Pepys (1633-1703) is said to have visited the French ordinary and it's easy to imagine him in this atmospheric, historic setting. It would certainly have been convenient, as he was Secretary of the Admiralty at the Navy Office on adjacent Crutched Friars.

The splendidly-named Crutched Friars was named for the House of the Friars of the Holy Cross which stood here, *crux* being the Latin for cross.

19. Great St Helens & St Helen's Place, EC2

Transport: Bank tube or Liverpool Street tube/rail

This is one of the City's more attractive corners, surrounding one of its oldest and loveliest churches, the twin-naved St Helen's Bishopsgate. The church dates from at least the 13th century, perhaps earlier. It's even claimed that it was built on the site of a pagan temple by Constantine when he converted to Christianity in the 4th century, although there's little evidence to support this.

The church is sometimes called the City's Westminster Abbey and is second only to the Abbey in terms of its number of memorials, including the tomb of Sir Thomas Gresham, founder of the Royal Exchange. There's also a memorial to Sir John Crosby, buried here in 1475. Crosby Hall, his home, stood nearby and 500 years later was moved, brick by brick, to Chelsea and reassembled (see Paultons Square & Danvers Street on page 176).

The church has been much altered since the 13th century and was restored in 1994-7 following IRA bombings in 1992 and 1993 (in St Mary Axe and Bishopsgate, respectively). Today the church and the tranquil area surrounding it form a relaxing, low-lying enclave in this vibrant, high-rise part of the City.

Norman Foster's iconic Gherkin sits behind St Helen's Bishopsgate, seeming to emerge from its roof, an intriguing juxtaposition of the very old and the cutting-edge new.

20. Great Swan Alley, EC2

Transport: Moorgate tube/rail

Leading off Coleman Street, pedestrians-only Great Swan Alley is mainly covered and without much of interest at its western end. But stick with it and cross Moorgate, where the second section of the alley widens and is open to traffic. The main attraction here is the attractive, elegant Chartered Accountants' Hall, with its entrance on adjacent Moorgate Place.

> The alley is named after Ye Swan's Nest (once called the White Swan), a pub that was demolished in the 1860s.

Now home to the Institute of Chartered Accountants in England and Wales, the Hall was built in 1890-93 in neo-Baroque style by John Belcher, with an extension added in the '30s. It has decorative carved friezes in the middle and top of the building; the one above the first-floor windows shows a range of trades and professions, including over 100 figures.

Great Swan Alley is also notable for being the scene of an attempted insurrection in 1661 by the Fifth Monarchists, a sect that believed in biblical prophecy. They predicted that 1666 (the year of the great fire!) would see the end of man's domination on Earth, and planned to help bring this about by seizing power for Jesus using armed force. But after a couple of days of causing localised mayhem, the perpetrators were caught and their leaders hung, drawn and quartered.

Chartered Accountants' Hall

21. Guildhall Yard, EC2

Transport: Bank or St Paul's tube

Guildhall Yard is a large, airy space off Gresham Street, with its own unique atmosphere, history and layout and some comfortable benches from which to contemplate the surroundings. The Guildhall is easily the oldest and most important secular building in the City. It's been the administrative base of the Corporation of

the City of London for over 800 years; the name comes from its initial function as a place where *geld* (money) was collected as tax. The Guildhall was the centre of civic government and where Lord Mayors and Sheriffs were elected and council meetings held. It was also used for important trials and cultural events.

The Polish composer Chopin gave his last public performance at the Guildhall and it's where the UK's most significant literary award, the Man Booker Prize, is presented.

The impressive building is a mixture of the old and new. There's been a Guildhall here since at least 1128, and probably since the time of Edward the Confessor (reigned 1043-66). It was rebuilt from 1411 and much of the structure remains from then; the western crypt is thought to be late 13th century or earlier. The complex suffered damage in the Great Fire and the Blitz, but the medieval parts of the Old Hall survived remarkably well.

Adjacent is the Guildhall Art Gallery (below), a semi-Gothic stone construction, intended to be sympathetic to its neighbour.

Beneath the gallery sits a gem: in 1988, the Museum of London made one of its most significant archaeological discoveries when it unearthed London's only Roman amphitheatre (above). The City of London was keen to integrate the remains into its plans for a new art gallery, so excavations and building work took place at the same time. The amphitheatre's remains are now displayed under the gallery in a controlled environment, including digital technology, atmospheric lighting and sound effects.

A circular band of black paving stones in Guildhall Yard marks the full outline of the amphitheatre, thought to be the largest in Roman Britain.

The Gallery is home to the City of London's art collection and displays around 250 works at any one time (out of a total of some 4,500). The collection dates from the 17th century onwards and includes works by Constable, Landseer, Millais and Rossetti.

Opposite the Guildhall is the church of St Lawrence Jewry (below), which is Grade I listed and has a pretty water garden in front. The first church here was erected in 1136 and named after St Lawrence, a deacon of Rome who was executed in 258 AD; it was rebuilt by Wren in 1671-77. Jewry refers to the area of the City (around modern-day Old Jewry) that was set aside for Jews before they were expelled from England in 1291.

22. Lothbury, EC2

Transport: Bank tube

The origin of Lothbury's name is unknown. It may come from lod, a drain or cut leading into a larger stream, the Walbrook in this instance. Or it might derive from the personal name Lod, short for the extravagantly-named Albertus Loteringus, a canon of St Paul's at the time of the Norman Conquest.

> Lothbury could also have developed from Lottenbury, a place where founders cast candlesticks and other copper items; founders were certainly here in the early Middle Ages.

By the early 18th century, merchants and bankers had moved in and Lothbury now runs behind the Bank of England. The attractive St Margaret Lothbury sits opposite the Bank. There's been a church here since 1181 or 1197 (sources vary) and the current example is by Wren and dates from 1686-90, with a nicely-proportioned interior. Of particular note is the baptismal font by the renowned carver Grinling Gibbons (1648-1721).

Next to the church is stylish 7 Lothbury, with very narrow, gated passageways (St Margaret's Close and Tokenhouse Yard) on either side. Number 7 was designed by G. S. Clarke the Elder in 1866 and is the City's best example of Victorian Gothic architecture. The pink and white colours of the exterior result from mixing different-coloured stones rather than using paint or stucco, and the building also has interesting carved and sculpted detail.

St Margaret Lothbury

7 Lothbury

23. Lovat Lane, EC3

Transport: Monument tube

Narrow, winding Lovat Lane runs south from Eastcheap, its entrance facing the distinctive 33-35 Eastcheap (below). This building divides opinion: some see it as a remarkable Gothic brick confection, others as an ugly, over-the-top carbuncle. It's by Robert Louis Roumieu and was built in 1868 as a wine and vinegar warehouse on the site of the famous Boar's Head Tavern, where Shakespeare's Falstaff was a regular.

A green sign below the Lovat Lane street sign states 'To St Mary-at-Hill, a Famous Wren Church'. This attractive little church was founded in the 12th century, rebuilt in the 15th and built again by Wren after the Great Fire. There are Dutch influences in the design and the interior is reputed to be one of the City's most attractive.

> St Mary-at-Hill's official entrance is on the street of the same name, and it's usually open all day on Tuesdays, Wednesdays and Thursdays.

Lovat Lane used to be called Love Lane, probably because it was frequented by prostitutes. The name was changed in 1939 to avoid confusion with another Love Lane in the City (EC2). It's Dickensian in atmosphere, although as you stroll south, the ultra-modern Shard appears ahead, framed by buildings on either side. At the bottom of the lane is a Nicholson's pub, The Walrus and Carpenter (a Lewis Carroll reference).

24. Mason's Avenue, EC2

Transport: Moorgate tube/rail

Linking Basinghall Street with Coleman Street, Mason's Avenue is a narrow walkway, covered at both ends, which conjures up the atmosphere of the old City rather than the new. It's easy to overlook but well known to workers from the area's numerous offices as the site of a convivial if oddly-named pub, The Old Dr Butler's Head (open Mon-Fri, 11am-11pm).

Mason's Avenue was named for the Worshipful Company of Masons, whose livery hall was located here from 1410-1865.

There's been a pub here since around 1610, although much of what we see today is more recent. It's named after a Dr William Butler, who wangled himself a position as James I's court physician, despite being a quack with no medical training. Among other creative 'cures', Butler developed his own medicinal ale which proved to be rather popular, and drinking establishments selling this brew were required to display his portrait.

Today, The Old Dr Butler's Head (below) is owned by the noted Kent brewer Shepherd Neame and has a Dickensian ambience, being gas-lit and wood-panelled. It also offers the opportunity to drink outside in the traffic-free Mason's Avenue.

25. Mincing Lane, EC3

Transport: Fenchurch Street tube/rail

The intriguingly named Mincing Lane, which links Fenchurch Street and Great Tower Street, has nothing to do with gentlemen who are more in touch with their feminine side. Rather it gets its name from a superfluity of nuns. Mincing is a corruption of the word *mynchens*, from the Benedictine nuns (or *mynchens*) of St Helen's Bishopsgate, who held property here. *Mynchen* comes from *minicen*, Anglo-Saxon for nun.

Despite its earlier religious connections, by the 19th century Mincing Lane was at the heart of the City's drugs trade, notably opium. Charles Dickens refers to this in *Our Mutual Friend*: '...arrived in the drug-flavoured region of Mincing Lane, with the sensation of having just opened a drawer in a chemist's shop'. Today, it's mainly home to insurance companies, many of which are housed in the monolithic Minster Court, a complex of three office buildings erected in the early '90s.

Three large (over 3m tall) bronze horses stand in the forecourt of Minster Court. Sculpted by Althea Wynne, they're nicknamed Dollar, Yen and Sterling.

Designed by GMW Partnership, Minster Court (left) is a blend of Art Deco and Gothic – the style has been called postmodern-Gothic – and is nicknamed Dracula's Castle. The exterior appears in the 1996 Disney film *101 Dalmatians* as Cruella De Vil's haute couture fashion house.

26. Puma Court, E1

Transport: Aldgate East tube or Shoreditch High Street rail

Across the road from Spitalfields Market, historic Puma Court leads east away from traffic-plagued Commercial Street, providing a charming, car-free backwater in this busy corner of Spitalfields. Three traditional street lamps add to the sense of bygone times but the main draw is a group of eight almshouses, which have an understated charm.

> Puma Court used to be called Red Lion Court as it abutted Red Lion Street to the west, and is first mentioned in the 1600s. The reason for the name change is unknown.

Compact and stylish, they're constructed from lovely old brick with pale green, wooden window shutters. They were built in 1860 'for poor inhabitants of the Liberty of Norton Folgate in place of those built in 1728 lately taken down for the New Street', as a helpful sign on the front relates.

The Liberty of Norton Folgate was an area of the City from which the king received no revenues. One of the various legacies bequeathed to Britain by the long period of the Middle Ages (which lasted from the 5th to 15th century), a 'liberty' refers to an area in which regalian rights are revoked and land is held by a feudal lord instead – thus the land and its income are in private, not royal hands. The Liberty of Norton Folgate was situated between the Bishopsgate ward to the south, the parish of St Leonard,

Almshouses

Shoreditch to the north and the parish of Spitalfields to the east. It was one of many such areas in London which did not pay dues to the monarchy.

> The existence of the Liberty of Norton Folgate became known to a much wider public when the ska/pop band Madness used it as the title for their critically acclaimed 2009 concept album.

The name Norton Folgate dates back a thousand years. Norton is recorded as early as around 1110 as *Nortune*, i.e. north farmstead, while Folgate might come from the manorial family name *Foliot* – or from *Foldweg*, the Saxon term for a highway, probably referring to Ermine Street, the Roman road that ran through the area. The liberty became part of Whitechapel in 1855 and existed until 1900.

It's a fascinating area to wander around, and its history is remembered in a street called Norton Folgate, which connects Bishopsgate and Shoreditch High Street just north of Liverpool Street Station.

27. St Alphage Garden & Salters' Garden, EC2

Transport: Barbican tube or Moorgate tube/rail

St Alphage Garden is a passage off Wood Street that leads to a small garden of the same name. The garden is built on the eponymous church's former graveyard, named for St Alfege, 29th Archbishop of Canterbury, who was careless enough to be beaten to death by Vikings at Greenwich in 1012.

The garden is right by a substantial section of Roman and medieval wall, and steps lead down to the larger, more interesting Salters' Garden, which is on the other side of the wall. This second garden is behind Salters' Hall, whose front is on Fore Street, opposite the Barbican. It's a modern knot garden, an unexpected haven of calm with elegant planting, benches and tinkling fountains. Salters' Garden is often closed. but you can view it through the gate and also from the open area under the Hall.

The Salters' Company (see page 111) was established in 1394 and has had a number of halls. The current one was designed by Sir Basil Spence and opened in 1976. Salt was a vital commodity in medieval times, used for the preservation of fish and meat, and was imported from western France and distributed by the Company's salters.

Salters' Garden

The importance of salt dates back to the Romans. The salt ration they received – the *sal* – is the basis of the word salary.

28. St Dunstan's Alley & Hill, EC3

Transport: Fenchurch Street tube/rail

St Dunstan's Hill runs south from Great Tower Street and, together with St Dunstan's Alley, embraces one of the loveliest of the City's gardens. The garden of St Dunstan-in-the-East (below and right) has grown in and around the shell of the church which once stood here – a wild yet tranquil green space offering respite from the busy Square Mile.

St Dunstan was a Saxon Archbishop of Canterbury in the 10th century and has two City churches named after him: St Dunstan-in-the-East and St Dunstan-in-the-West, which still stands on Fleet Street. The church here dates from Saxon times. Damaged in the Great Fire, it was rebuilt by Sir Christopher Wren in 1697, but only the tower and some of the walls survived the Blitz. The tower has housed a complementary medical clinic since 1990.

> St Dunstan's garden is open daily from 8am to 7pm or dusk. It's a popular lunchtime perch for workers from nearby offices, so is best visited during mornings, evenings or at weekends.

Around the tower and within the ruined nave, the grandly-named Worshipful Company of Gardeners has laid out a beautiful garden, with benches, trees and small areas of lawn. It's spread over two levels, with clever planting clinging to the walls and weaving in and out of the windows – it's one corner of the concrete City which nature has reclaimed.

29. St Olave's Court, EC2

Transport: Bank tube

St Olave's Court is a turning off Old Jewry and is one of the many attractive alleys, courts and lanes that characterise this part of the City (see also Frederick's Place on page 137). It has a narrow, covered entrance and is named after one of the three London churches dedicated to King Olaf Haroldsson (995-1030), a Norwegian who fought the Danes in London and who was later canonised.

The church on this spot was called St Olave Upwell Old Jewry (the first one was built in the mid-12th century) and was named after a well in the churchyard. It was demolished in 1888 under the Union of City Benefices Act (1860), which brought the number of churches in line with the shrinking population. The tower was left standing for some reason and it used to serve as the rectory for St Margaret Lothbury.

The western end of St Olave's Court joins Ironmonger Lane, so-called because of the ironmongers who traded here until the late 16th century.

Today the tower (occupied by a company of solicitors) has a small garden in front on part of what was the church's graveyard; its greenery adds to the tranquillity of this attractive, car-free corner of old London.

30. St Peter's Alley, EC3

Transport: Bank tube

Narrow and often overlooked, St Peter's Alley doglegs around the church of St Peter upon Cornhill. It has two entrances: a narrow one on Cornhill that's easy to miss, and another on Gracechurch Street to the left of a branch of Ede and Ravenscroft, London's oldest tailor (1689).

> St Peter upon Cornhill is now a Christian study centre. Note the attractive, decorative figure of St Peter atop the Victorian entrance gates to the garden.

The church is reputed to have been founded in 179AD on the site of London's Roman basilica by Lucius, the first Christian King of Britain, although this is probably wishful thinking and the first reference to a church here isn't until 1040. The present building is by Sir Christopher Wren, built 1675-81, and its small, mainly paved garden is a relatively peaceful spot in this busy part of the City, the benches popular with office workers and the odd vagrant.

The garden is on the site of the church's (raised) graveyard, which appears in Charles Dickens's *Our Mutual Friend*, playfully described as 'conveniently and healthily elevated above the living'. Burials ceased here in 1850 and the graveyard was later converted into a public garden.

31. Sandy's Row & Artillery Passage, E1

Transport: Liverpool Street tube/rail

Sandy's Row leads off Artillery Lane (see page 118) and is part of an engaging tangle of historic, meandering thoroughfares that sits behind busy Bishopsgate. The origin of its name is uncertain, but Sandy may have been a prominent resident or even the man who built the houses on this street.

This characterful thoroughfare is most notable for an attractive building that's now the Sandy's Row Synagogue, above (tel. 020-8883 4169 for details of tours). Grade II listed, it dates from around 1766 and was probably once a Huguenot chapel, thereafter passing through the hands of various denominations, in line with the area's changing population. It was acquired by the Jewish community in 1854 and formally consecrated as a synagogue in 1870.

Bishopsgate takes its name from one of the original eight Roman city gates, which was rebuilt many times and finally demolished in 1760. In Tudor times it was lined with the houses of the wealthy and is now dominated by skyscrapers – realms of the City's 21st-century rich.

It's the oldest Ashkenazi synagogue in London (the Ashkenazi Jews once lived along the Rhine in Germany) and one of only a handful of synagogues remaining in the East End of London where there were once over 100. Opposite the synagogue is another attractive, original building: number 4 Sandy's Row was once a private house but is now home to a property agency.

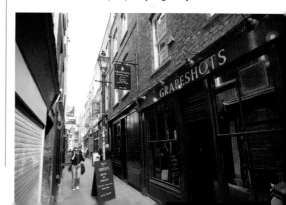

Artillery Passage runs east off Sandy's Row. This narrow walkway recalls the London of two or three centuries ago and is one of those places where you can imagine coming face to face with Mr Pickwick or Uriah Heep – or even Dickens himself!

Locals used to know Artillery Passage as Tasel Close, named after the prickly teazles (or tasels) used by Huguenot weavers to comb and prepare cloth.

At the junction between Artillery Passage and Sandy's Row is a bar and dining room called Grapeshots (below and previous page), which is owned by the Davy's chain of wine bars. Grapeshot is a type of shot made of a mass of small metal balls and the name is a reminder of this area's military past (see Artillery Lane on page 118). Other buildings in this fascinating passage are home to a selection of small shops, eateries and upmarket tailors.

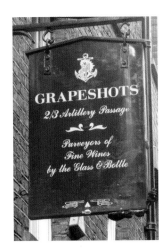

32. Star Alley, EC3

Transport: Fenchurch Street tube/rail

Bridging the gap between Mark Lane and Fenchurch Street, Star Alley is home to the remnants of All Hallows Staining. The alley is named after a tavern, now long gone, and all that remains of the church is its small but well-preserved tower. Its name is unusual: 'stain' (or stone) may have been added to the church's name to distinguish it from other City churches dedicated to St Hallows, which were probably made of wood. Or it may have been named after the manor of Staines.

The tower dates from the 14th or 15th century and has long outlasted the rest of the church which was rebuilt after the Great Fire but collapsed in 1671, allegedly due to too many burials around its walls. It was rebuilt again, then demolished in 1870. Beneath the churchyard is a 12th-century crypt which was moved here in 1825 from Monkswell Street, where it had been part of a Cripplegate hermitage (religious retreat).

The crypt had been acquired in 1548 by a William Lambe (it still carries his name) and when he died in 1577 he left it to the Worshipful Company of Clothworkers, of whom he'd been master. Today, both tower and crypt are maintained by the Company.

Gothic Minster Court (see Mincing Lane on page 146) can be seen behind the tower, making an interesting contrast between old and new.

33. Throgmorton Avenue, EC2

Transport: Bank tube

The curiously named Throgmorton Avenue is a private road running between London Wall and Throgmorton Street, once home to the London Stock Exchange. In earlier times it was the site of an important Augustinian Priory and Thomas Cromwell, the man responsible for implementing Henry VIII's policy of dissolving such monasteries (and the King's chief minister), built his palace here.

> Both thoroughfares are named after Nicholas Throckmorton (c1515-71), politician, banker and Elizabeth I's Ambassador to France and Scotland.

The fearsome Cromwell attracted the dislike of his neighbours by encroaching on their properties in order to extend his garden, but there was nothing they could do against such a powerful man who, some say, was the effective ruler of England. But after Cromwell's fall from grace (he was executed in 1540), the Worshipful Company of Drapers bought the property to use as their Hall, and it still dominates tranquil Throgmorton Avenue today.

There was an association of drapers as early as the 12th century and the Company received its first charter in 1364. The wool trade was of great significance in medieval England and the drapers became influential and wealthy. The elegant frontage of Drapers' Hall runs along much of Throgmorton Avenue, with a garden at the junction with Copthall Avenue (it's private but can be viewed through the railings).

Drapers' Hall

34. Trinity Square & Gardens, EC3

Transport: Tower Hill tube

Sometimes overlooked in favour of nearby attractions – notably the Tower of London – this is a curious corner of the City. Trinity Square is home to the former headquarters of the Port of London Authority, built in 1912-22 in showy Edwardian style by Sir Edwin Cooper. Next to it is small, elegant Trinity House, built in 1792-4, which houses the central authority that governs lighthouses around the coasts of England and Wales.

Both face on to Trinity Gardens, a large green space which has at its centre a memorial to merchant seamen and fishermen lost at sea during the two World Wars. Their names are inscribed on a series of plaques: 12,000 names from the First World War, 24,000 from the Second. The First World War section of the memorial was designed by Sir Edwin Lutyens, with sculptures by Sir William Reid-Dick, while the one commemorating the Second World War was designed by Sir Edward Maufe, with sculptures by Charles Wheeler. It's a poignant tribute to those who have 'no grave but the sea'.

Trinity Gardens' more gruesome heritage is marked by a stone where a scaffold once stood. It was used for beheading traitors and lawbreakers outside the Tower of London (only the highest-class felons were executed *inside* the Tower) and more than 125 met their end on this spot.

CHAPTER 4

WEST & SOUTHWEST LONDON

1. Bathurst Mews, W2

Transport: Lancaster Gate tube or Paddington tube/rail

Tucked away behind Lancaster Gate, linking Bathurst Street with Sussex Place, Bathurst Mews is a cobbled enclave: tranquil, authentic and impressive. The section just off Bathurst Place is short, but swing right to enjoy a long, straight line of attractive mews houses, some of which have changed little over the last few centuries.

Mews is a term for a row of stables and carriage houses, with living quarters above, built around a paved court or along a street. They were constructed behind London's larger houses in the 17th and 18th centuries, so are invariably located in wealthier areas, and most have been converted into fashionable homes.

The term 'mews' comes from a building where falcons were kept; the birds' cyclical loss of feathers is known as 'mewing' (moulting).

It isn't only the rich and privileged who live in Bathurst Mews. Ross Nye Stables is located here – so Bathurst even smells like an original city mews. In fact, this is the last London mews in which horses are still stabled today. It was founded in 1965, with rides taking place in nearby Hyde Park. The stables are open Tue-Sun (see http://rossnyestables.co.uk for details), but are closed in late July and August so that the horses can have a 'holiday'.

2. Campden Hill Square, W8

Transport: Holland Park tube

Rising south of where Notting Hill Gate morphs into Holland Park Avenue, Campden Hill Square is built on the slope of Campden Hill (named for the Campden House Estate), with commanding views over the surrounding area. Indeed, the artist J M W Turner (1775-1851) painted sunsets from here, which is commemorated by a plaque on a tree in the central (private) garden.

Built in 1827-38 by J F Hanson, Campden Hill Square was called Notting Hill Square until 1893, when residents campaigned for a name change. It's attractive, quiet and prosperous, with quirky, old-fashioned lampposts, and is surrounded by high, handsome terraces in a variety of styles – no bland uniformity here. Unusually, the houses have their own small front gardens, in addition to the communal central garden.

Campden Hill Square has a number of blue plaques: on number 9 to John McDouall Stuart, the first explorer to cross Australia; on number 16 to Charles Morgan, novelist and critic; on number 23 to Siegfried Sassoon, one of the leading poets of World War One; while number 50 commemorates Evelyn Underhill, Christian philosopher and teacher.

Camden Hill Square was the UK's most desirable – and expensive – street in 2011, according to a survey by Lloyds TSB. In 2015 the average price for a house was just over £8m (Zoopla).

3. Chelsea Square, SW3

Transport: South Kensington tube

Nestling at the heart of this characterful, upmarket part of London, Chelsea Square is surrounded by a number of streets and passages that also bear exploring. The square itself is large, with an extensive, private central garden. Many of the surrounding buildings are classic red-brick three-storey terraces.

Most interesting are the eye-catching detached properties towards the southwest of the square. Numbers 40 and 41 are especially striking; sleek and white, they date from 1930 and 1934 and have a shared garden. The houses are by the English architect and garden designer Oliver Hill (1887-1968) who was initially a follower of

> The garden at the centre of Chelsea Square may be a small remnant of Chelsea Common which once extended to over 30 acres.

the Arts & Crafts style, and later (from the '30s onwards) an exponent of modernism.

Chelsea Square was once called Trafalgar Square. When London County Council renamed a number of streets in the '20s to avoid titular repetition, the oldest ones generally kept their original names, but this was an exception. The Trafalgar Square here is much older than the one near Charing Cross but the latter's fame meant that its name couldn't be changed.

4. Edwardes Square, W8

Transport: High Street Kensington or Kensington (Olympia) tube

Sitting south of Kensington High Street, Edwardes Square is noteworthy for its large (around 3 acres) and lush central garden. This dates from 1820 and was designed by an Italian artist, Agostino Alio, whose generous planting and winding walks make it different from most of London's other garden squares. There's even a Greek-style lodge with Doric columns for the gardener, known as 'the Temple' and still in use.

Adjacent to the north side of the square are the rear gardens of Earls Terrace, a row of beautifully restored Georgian houses facing Kensington High Street and said to be one of England's most expensive terraces.

The east and west sides of the square have low, original terraces – not mirrored, although both have taller houses in the centre – while the south of the square has a more modern mix of architecture.

Edwardes Square features a number of blue plaques: number 11 to author and humanist G Lowes Dickinson; number 19 to Italian poet Ugo Foscolo; and number 27 to actor and comedian Frankie Howerd. Other notable residents have included writers G K Chesterton, Leigh Hunt, Elizabeth Inchbald and George du Maurier.

> The square was built 1811-19 by Louis Leon Changeur and is named after William Edwardes, father of the landowner, the 2nd Lord Kensington.

5. Elvaston Mews, SW7

Transport: Gloucester Road tube

Elvaston Mews is one of several mews in this picturesque area south of Hyde Park. It's a traditional mews in all but its shape, which is in the form of a 't'. Its western entrance is just over Queen's Gate Place from Petersham Mews, another pretty, cobbled, pastel-coloured mews that's well worth exploring. The other entrance – a slightly over-the-top, twin-pillared affair – is on Elvaston Place, and the mews continues a short way to the north on the other side of the road.

Both Mews and Place derive their name from Elvaston Castle in Derbyshire, seat of the Earls of Harrington. The Harrington Estate was a large estate in South Kensington owned by the Stanhopes, Viscounts Petersham and Earls of Harrington, until it was sold by the 11th Earl in 1957.

Elvaston Place mainly comprises large, mid-Victorian properties, many of them now divided into flats, while others house embassies; number 27 is the Gabonese Embassy and number 32-33 is the Mauritius High Commission.

Number 32 Elvaston Place reputedly catered to a different kind of clientele in the '50s, when it's said to have housed London's best-run brothel.

6. Ennismore Gardens & Ennismore Gardens Mews, SW7

Transport: Knightsbridge tube

Ennismore Gardens is a sizeable garden square in what was once part of the Kingston House Estate. The private garden has some impressive trees and eye-catching planting, while the surrounding terraces display a variety of architectural styles.

> The American actress Ava Gardner (1922-90) lived at 34 Ennismore Gardens from 1968, and there's a memorial urn to her in the square.

The square's name derives from William Hare, Viscount Ennismore and Earl of Listowel, who purchased the estate in 1813. He died in 1837 and parts of the estate were later sold for redevelopment, including the Palladian Kingston House which was later replaced by '30s apartment blocks.

The attractive cream-painted terrace on the east side dates from 1843-46. Ennismore Mews (which leads off Ennismore Gardens) was built at the same time, and today is the site of a Russian Orthodox church. The north side of Ennismore Gardens was built from 1870, with large houses and mews behind them. It was unusual for houses built this late to be provided with decent mews and carriage houses (which was more common in the 17th and 18th centuries than the 19th).

Ennismore Gardens Mews, which runs south and west of Ennismore Gardens, is another smart cobbled mews with pretty pastel houses.

7. Ensor Mews & Cranley Mews, SW7

Transport: South Kensington tube

The section of Kensington between the Fulham Road and the cluster of fine museums to the south of Kensington Gore is well worth an aimless wander. You'll discover a network of interesting mews, meandering streets, intriguing side passages and impressive, leafy squares, many home to eye-catching, varied architecture.

Ensor Mews is one of these and is announced by a brick arch entrance off Cranley Gardens. The mews is cobbled and the houses are mainly original and painted a variety of pretty pastel shades. Two short spurs run off the main section of the mews – little oases of tranquillity.

In 2013, a house is Ensor Mews was on the market with Savills for just under £6m. Not bad for a home in a former stable block.

Nearby Cranley Mews runs north behind Cranley Gardens to join busy Brompton Road. It's longer and more substantial than the average mews, and many of the soft-hued houses are original. Cranley Mews carries more than a whiff of a high street in a small market town, which is remarkable in this hectic part of London. It helps to explain why mews living is so sought-after.

8. Godfrey Street, SW3

Transport: Sloane Square or South Kensington tube

Godfrey Street is quite possibly one of the capital's prettiest neighbourhoods. It's approached via Burnsall Street, just north of the King's Road, which is attractive in its own right. Its houses are painted in a variety of colours, which gives a clue of what to expect when you turn right into Godfrey Street.

Godfrey Street has the atmosphere of a large mews, although it isn't cobbled and lacks the carriage houses and stables, converted into garages, found in many mews. Instead it boasts rows of strikingly pretty artisans' cottages, making it a very desirable and exclusive address, although a glance at house prices in a local estate agent's window will almost certainly shatter any dreams of living here.

Look out for number 14 Burnsall Street, spanning just a few feet across and surely one of the narrowest houses in London.

The houses are in a variety of styles, mainly two-storey, but with some three-storey properties towards the end that leads into Cale Street. This thoroughfare is named for an 18th-century benefactress, Judith Cale, who made a bequest to 'six poor widows of Chelsea'.

9. Hesper Mews, SW5

Transport: Earl's Court tube

Hesper Mews is just east of Earl's Court Road, a turning off Bramhall Gardens. It has a more quirky variety of buildings than the majority of London mews, which tend to be fairly uniform. The mews was originally part of the Gunter Estate, whose buildings largely date from the period between 1865 and 1896, built on land owned by the brothers James and Robert Gunter. Previously the area was mainly used for – indeed, was famous for – garden cultivation.

Cobbled Hesper Mews is the largest and best of the estate's mews. Part of it is overlooked by the backs of the tall, red-brick houses which face onto an adjacent street, while the houses on the mews itself are a mixture of original and restored buildings in a variety of styles, some taller than others. And it isn't simply a straight line of houses, as three shallow courts lead off it.

The east end of Hesper Mews leads into Laverton Place. Cross the road to spot a blue plaque to Egyptologist Howard Carter (1874-1939), who discovered Tutankhamen's tomb.

This eye-catching, distinguished corner of the capital is full of small squares and streets which reward the intrepid explorer – and provides a tantalising glimpse of how the other half live.

10. Hyde Park Gardens Mews & Surrounds, W2

Transport: Lancaster Gate tube or Paddington tube/rail

Hyde Park Gardens Mews, linking Stanhope Terrace and Sussex Place with Clarendon Place, is a long, attractive, cobbled mews, with mainly original buildings, and is an atmospheric thoroughfare to wander along.

Watch out for horse droppings in these parts, as the mews is on the route used by Ross Nye Stables, based in nearby Bathurst Mews (see page 160).

South of the mews is Hyde Park Gardens – the two are linked by a covered passageway – which is interesting for the contrast in neighbouring properties. On the north side are the backs of the mews houses in Hyde Park Gardens Mews, while the south provides a view of the large imposing properties overlooking Bayswater Road and Hyde Park, including one that's home to the High Commission of Sri Lanka.

Hyde Park itself covers 340 acres and is the largest of the Royal Parks. It was one of three properties – Ebury, Hyde and Neate – that made up the Manor of Eia, bequeathed to the monks of Westminster soon after the Norman Conquest. Henry VIII later sold Ebury and Neate, keeping Hyde as a hunting ground. It was opened to the public in the early 1600s, although deer continued to be hunted in the park until 1768.

11. Kensington Church Walk, W8

Transport: High Street Kensington tube

Tucked away behind Kensington High Street, Kensington Church Walk is approached directly from the High Street next to the ornate Melli Bank building, or from Kensington Church Court via an archway next to St Mary Abbots Church. At the end of the court a shallow ramp leads down into the walk. Two tranquil gardens provide respite from the high street shopping frenzy: the Alec Clifton-Taylor Memorial Gardens and St Mary Abbots Gardens, once the church cemetery.

Church Walk curves past the attractive church before heading north to Holland Street. There's been a church on this site since around the 12th century. The current one was built 1869-72 in neo-Gothic Early English style by Sir George Gilbert Scott – also responsible for magnificent St Pancras Station – although it retains a number of fittings from

St Mary Abbots

earlier churches. It also has London's tallest spire (278ft/85m).

> Nearby Kensington Church Street, a mecca for antiques hunters, was once a country lane linking Kensington village with Notting Hill Gate.

Notable worshippers have included scientist Sir Isaac Newton, anti-slavery campaigner William Wilberforce and author Beatrix Potter. Prime Minister David Cameron is a regular attendee.

12. Kensington Square, W8

Transport: High Street Kensington tube

A short stroll southeast from High Street Kensington tube station, Kensington Square is an attractive, characterful enclave laid out in 1685 by Thomas Young, making it one of London's first garden squares.

Originally called King's Square, it became a fashionable place to live after William III converted nearby Nottingham House into Kensington Palace. It was surrounded by fields until around the middle of the 19th century. Many of the houses on the north, south and west sides are original, if generally much altered. The majority date from the period between the mid-1680s and the 1730s, which accounts for the interesting variety of styles.

Number 16 houses the Malta High Commission, number 17 has a blue plaque to the composer Hubert Parry (composer

of *Jerusalem*) and number 18 has a green plaque to the philosopher John Stuart Mill. There's a blue plaque on number 40 to the pioneer of public health Sir John Simon and one on number 41 (left) to the artist Sir Edward Burne-Jones. The square also boasts a church and nursery school.

> Sadly, the lush garden at the heart of Kensington Square is private, although it's possible to visit it during an Open Squares weekend (www.opensquares.org).

13. Kynance Mews, SW7

Transport: Gloucester Road or High Street Kensington tube

As befits its location in the grand Royal Borough of Kensington and Chelsea, Kynance Mews has its own entrance arches, on either side of Launceston Place. The mews is one of several in the area between Kensington High Street and Gloucester Road which was initially known as Kensington New Town, and is now sometimes called Victoria Road Village.

Part of the De Vere Conservation Area, Kynance Mews is cobbled and lined with original properties that were built as coach houses and stables for the grand mansions of Cornwall Gardens. It's widely regarded as

one of central London's most beautiful 19th-century mews developments (a competitive field) and a very desirable place to reside.

Interest and variety are added by diverse roof styles, plain and painted brickwork façades in different colours, raised party walls, seats, benches and a variety of planting, while halfway along 'secret' steps lead up to Christ Church Kensington. It's a haven of calm and has more than a hint of a rustic village transplanted into a busy part of the capital.

> We're lucky Kynance Mews survives intact, as the area to the south was almost completely destroyed by bombs during the winter of 1940.

14. Lansdowne Road & Ladbroke Walk, W11

Transport: Holland Park tube

Wide, elegant Lansdowne Road has a number of large villas in various styles, but one of the most eye-catching is Lansdowne House, on the corner of Ladbroke Road. This striking building, several storeys high, was designed by William Flockhart and built in 1904; it used to contain studios for struggling artists, as a blue plaque confirms, and more recently was a recording studio where the likes of John Lennon and Queen recorded. It now houses a dozen eye-wateringly expensive flats.

> As with many thoroughfares on the Ladbroke Estate, Lansdowne Road was named after a member of the House of Lords: Lord Lansdowne (1780-1863), Lord President of the Council.

but name; it's surprisingly tranquil despite running parallel to busy Holland Park Avenue. The houses are taller and wider than typical mews properties, with a number painted in the oft-seen pastel colours; number 16 is modernist in style.

The name Ladbroke, which crops up all over this area, comes from the Ladbroke Estate, which was developed hereabouts in the 1840s by James Weller Ladbroke on land his family owned in north Kensington.

Walk east along Ladbroke Road and turn right down Ladbroke Grove, and Ladbroke Walk is the first turning on the left. This road is attractive, cobbled and a mews in all

15. Montpelier Square, SW7

Transport: Knightsbridge tube

Located midway between Brompton Road and Knightsbridge, Montpelier Square is the heart of the Montpelier Estate. The houses around the square's private central garden date from around 1824 and were originally designed as homes for the middle classes; several were lodging houses. When the square's stock rose, along with that of Knightsbridge generally, the upper classes began to move in. By the '30s, the local authority described Montpelier as the district's best residential square.

> The origin of the name is uncertain. An attractive (if fanciful) theory suggests that this then-rural part of London was reputed to have healthy air and was compared with the French resort of Montpellier.

Montpelier Square has had some well-known residents. Politician Anthony Barber (1920-2005) lived at number 15; he became the first person to be a member of both the House of Commons and House of Lords. Author Arthur Koestler (1905-83) lived at number 8; he and his wife committed suicide in the property when he was diagnosed with a terminal illness. And actress Leslie Caron (born 1931) lived at number 31 in the '60s.

Some other well-known inhabitants of Montpelier Square didn't actually exist. John Galsworthy chose 62 Montpelier Square as the fictional home of Soames Forsyte in his literary series *The Forsyte Saga*, published 1906-21.

16. Observatory Gardens, W8

Transport: High Street Kensington or Notting Hill Gate tube

Campden Hill Court

Situated midway between Holland Park and Kensington Gardens, Observatory Gardens leads off the long and varied stretch of Campden Hill Road. One side of the gardens houses a line of showy, red-brick terraces with white-pillared entrances, while the opposite side is taken up by a large residential block, Campden Hill Court, which faces on to Campden Hill Road.

> Sir James South had his own observatory in his back garden – the elevated position makes it ideal for star-gazing – which boasted the largest telescope in the world at the time.

There's no garden to speak of – just a number of modestly-sized trees – but at number 13 you'll find the handsome Observatory Lodge, and on railings opposite is a rectangular blue plaque that explains the 'observatory' part of the street's name. From 1826-67 the lodge was owned by Sir James South (it was he who renamed it Observatory House), a founding member of The Royal Astronomical Society.

Construction of Observatory Gardens began in 1870 on the site of New Campden House. This had previously been called Phillimore House, having been built in 1762 by Robert Phillimore (land hereabouts was part of the Phillimore Estate).

17. Paultons Square & Danvers Street, SW3

Transport: South Kensington tube

Paultons Square lies between lively King's Road (which forms its north side) and traffic-heavy Cheyne Walk, which runs along the north bank of the Thames in Chelsea. It was built on a former market garden in the 1830s and is named after Paultons in Hampshire, the country seat of George Stanley, son-in-law of physicist and collector Sir Hans Sloane (this area was part of the Sloane Stanley Estate).

It's a Georgian square, rectangular in shape, unexpectedly large in this built-up part of town, and mainly surrounded by low, original terraces. There's a welcome air of tranquillity, despite the buzz of the surrounding area. The east and west sides of the square are matching terraces, which are built slightly higher in the centre. The central garden is private and has some attractive, colourful planting and a number of large trees.

Number 9 has a blue plaque to the naturalist and writer Gavin Maxwell. Other well-known past residents include playwright Samuel Beckett and novelist Jean Rhys.

Leading south off Paultons Square is Danvers Street. Here, a blue plaque on number 20 (a large, cream-coloured, detached building) commemorates Sir Alexander Fleming, who discovered penicillin. But the most interesting building is at the south end of the street, on the corner with Cheyne Walk. Grade II listed medieval Crosby Hall can make a strong claim to be London's ultimate architectural moveable feast: it once

stood in Bishopsgate and was moved to Chelsea stone-by-stone in 1910 to save it from demolition.

Crosby Hall has been described by English Heritage as 'London's most important surviving secular domestic medieval building'.

The house was built in the City in 1466-75 by wool merchant Sir John Crosby, and was occupied by Richard III in 1483 when he was the Duke of Gloucester (it's mentioned in Shakespeare's play as the location of Gloucester's plotting). Sir Thomas More owned the property from 1532-4 and Sir Walter Raleigh lodged there in 1601. After a fire in 1672, only the Great Hall and Parlour wing survived, and it's these elements that make up the Chelsea 'house' we see today.

Crosby Hall is now a private house. It was purchased in 1989 by the controversial City businessman Christopher Moran, who's been barred for life by Lloyd's of London and censured by the London Stock Exchange. He's since been engaged in a long-running, restoration project, whose completion date keeps being extended.

18. Penzance Place & Surrounds, W11

Transport: Holland Park tube

Penzance Place, St James's Gardens and adjacent Addison Avenue comprise an attractive, upmarket corner of Holland Park which merits exploration. Heading east across Princedale Road and Pottery Lane (see page 180), Penzance Place meanders left to reveal picturesque rows of pastel-coloured three-storey houses, with wrought ironwork around the basements.

Addison Avenue is named after the essayist and statesman Joseph Addison, who lived at Holland House in Holland Park (the house was badly damaged in World War Two, although parts remain).

Retrace your steps to St James's Gardens, an understated garden square dating from the 1840s and built on the site of St James's Church. The gardens themselves are private, laid out in an informal woodland style, with a number of chestnut and lime trees. Heading south from here, Addison Avenue – also built in the 1840s – has attractive, pastel-hued paired houses in a variety of designs.

A little further on, the road swings left again and ends in a small paved area with benches, around which cluster some upmarket shops and a restaurant. It's a very desirable, tranquil spot, and adjacent Clarendon Cross and Portland Road boast more attractive terraces.

19. Porchester Terrace, W2

Transport: Bayswater or Queensway tube

Porchester Terrace leads north from Bayswater Road near the Kensington Thistle Hotel. It was Bayswater's first terrace and its buildings have a variety of architectural styles, some modern and bland, but many older and quirkier, including a number of original villas.

Number 3-5 at the southern end has an eye-catching small dome and a blue plaque to the prominent horticulturalists John and Jane Loudon. John built the villa in the 1820s

– it's a prototype of the suburban semi and originally consisted of two houses – and tended many varieties of plant in the garden. There are rather fewer plants today but it has a number of exotic-looking trees. It was John Loudon who recommended the use of the hardy and now ubiquitous plane trees in London's squares and streets.

> Porchester was one of the Hampshire estates of the Thistlewaite family, lessees of the Bishop of London's land in Paddington since the early 18th century.

Walking north, you pass attractive Fulton Mews on the left and then Queensborough Passage; look out for the small decorative friezes above the door of number 38. Several famous folk have lived in Porchester Terrace, including painters John Linnell and William Collins (father of writer Wilkie Collins) and the 1st Viscount Samuel.

20. Pottery Lane & Surrounds, W11

Transport: Holland Park tube

Once part of west London's most notorious slum, the area around Pottery Lane and Portland Road, running north from traffic-heavy Holland Park Avenue, is now as genteel as can be: a potpourri of pretty houses, upmarket shops and elegant eateries.

The houses in Pottery Lane are less grand than those that dominate Portland Road and resemble those found in a typical mews. Around a third are painted in pastel colours and some have the carriage houses and garages usually associated with mews houses. Further north along Pottery Lane are some taller properties and, after it crosses Penzance Place (see page 178), there are more attractive, mews-like houses and, at the top, the Church of St Francis of Assisi.

North of the church is Walmer Road, and on the right, opposite the gates to Avondale Park, is an eye-catching ancient kiln (right). It's a curious feature on a residential road and a nod to the area's industrial history.

Bottle kilns hark back to the early 19th century when Notting Hill's soft clay was fired into bricks, drainpipes, pots and tiles to serve the house-building boom; hence the name Pottery Lane.

The rectangular blue plaque on the front states that it's one of London's few remaining examples of a bottle kiln.

In the mid-19th century, the potters were joined by pig farmers who had been evicted from the Marble Arch area and these trades, coupled with a lack of sanitation, clean water or adequate planning, turned the area into an infamous slum which became known as the 'Potteries and the Piggeries'.

> Extraction of the clay left huge holes which became filled with stagnant water, pig slurry and sewage. One of these pools grew so large that it was known as 'The Ocean' – it was filled in 1892 and is now Avondale Park.

Some of the slum's inhabitants left a lot to be desired: the pig keepers were thought to be respectable but the brick makers were described as 'notorious types', known for 'riotous living'. In 1850, Charles

Dickens wrote that the area was 'a plague spot scarcely equalled for its insalubrity by any other in London' and some referred to Pottery Lane as 'Cut-throat Lane'. This is quite a contrast with today, when Notting Hill is home to some of the capital's financial, media and political elite, and houses sell for seven-figure sums.

Church of St Francis of Assisi

21. Queen's Gate Mews, SW7

Transport: Gloucester Road or High Street Kensington tube

Queen's Gate Mews is tucked away off busy Palace Gate, which houses a number of embassies and high commissions. The short, part-cobbled entrance doglegs right, then left as it enters the longest stretch of the mews.

It's a traditional, tranquil mews, bordered on one side by the rear of tall houses fronting the adjacent street, while along the other side are classic mews houses. Three short courts run off the mews, while at the end of the main section there's a civilised pub, The Queen's Arms (Mon-Sat noon-11pm; Sun noon-10.30pm). From here you can turn left (a dead end) or right down to Queen's Gate Terrace.

The pub's proximity to the Royal Albert Hall means that it's popular with regulars at the Proms. It also draws custom from the Royal College of Music, students from Imperial College and staff from the nearby museums. It boasts a decent selection of beer, which changes regularly, and good food (from burgers to gastro fare).

> Students from the Royal College of Music apparently know The Queen's Arms as 'The Nines', as the college has 98 practice rooms and the pub is regarded as the 99th.

22. Redcliffe Square & Mews, SW10

Transport: West Brompton tube

Redcliffe Square isn't one square but two, divided by Redcliffe Gardens. On the eastern side is a tree-festooned garden square, open to the public, while St Luke's Church dominates the western section. The surrounding houses are mainly constructed of light brick, many of them fronted by two-pillared porticos.

Linking the Fulham and Old Brompton Roads in the Royal Borough of Kensington and Chelsea, Redcliffe Gardens used to go by the decidedly Beatrix Potter-like name of Walnut Tree Walk. The name was changed when it became part of the Redcliffe Estate, which was developed from the 1860s by builders Alexander and McClymont on land owned by the Gunter family. Before this the area was mainly farmland.

> St Luke's dates from 1883 and was built by the Godwin brothers; the exterior is made of Kentish ragstone with Bath stone dressings, and contrasts with the plainer interior.

Attractive Harcourt Terrace leads off Redcliffe Square, and a right-hand turn takes you through a white gateway into Redcliffe Mews. The date 1869 is written above the name, although curiously the second entrance, further along Harcourt Terrace, is dated 1985. This suggests that not all the houses are original, and though cobbled and attractive, the mews has a more modern atmosphere than some.

23. Tedworth Square, SW3

Transport: Sloane Square tube

Tedworth Square sits in the distinguished district between the King's Road and Royal Hospital Road, with Tite Street running southeast from it. It has a central private garden, surrounded on three sides by characterful, original, red-brick terraces; the fourth side has a bland modern block.

The square is noted for its well-known past residents. Number 15 (now a subdivided rebuild) was the home of two actresses, though not at the same time: Lillie Langtry (1853-1929), sometime mistress of the Prince of Wales – later Edward VII – the Earl of Shrewsbury and Prince Louis of Battenberg, and Mrs Patrick Campbell (1865-1940), who had a passionate, albeit unconsummated, relationship with George Bernard Shaw which included a famous exchange of letters. Later, number 15 was the home of cricketer Sir Pelham (Plum) Warner (1873-1963).

There's a blue plaque on number 23 to American writer Samuel Clemens, better known as Mark Twain (1835-1910), who lived here 1896-97.

Tedworth Square got its name (rather circuitously) from the daughter-in-law of William Sloane-Stanley of Paultons who hailed from Tedworth (or Tidworth) in Hampshire. Paultons was a Hampshire country seat related to the Sloane Estate – see Paultons Square on page 176.

24. Wellington Square, SW3

Transport: Sloane Square tube

Wellington Square is the smallest and probably the most appealing of the squares off the King's Road. Built in around 1830 on land that had been one of the area's numerous garden nurseries, it was named after the nation's most revered military leader, the Duke of Wellington (1769-1852). Appropriately, his body lay in state at the nearby Royal Hospital before burial at St Paul's, and the Duke's brother was rector of Chelsea from 1805-36.

Wellington Square has attracted an interesting variety of notable residents over the years. The artist Charles Edward Conder (1868-1909), a friend of Toulouse-Lautrec, lived at number 14 in 1902, while the art critic James Laver (1899-1975) occupied number 11 in the '50s. US novelist Thomas Clayton Wolfe (1900-38) lived at number 32 in 1926 and AA Milne (1882-1956), creator of Winnie the Pooh, lodged at number 8 for a time (when it was owned by a policeman).

Aleister Crowley was denounced in the popular press as 'the great beast' and 'the wickedest man alive', although he delighted in such epithets.

The square's most notorious resident was the English writer, mountaineer, occultist and self-publicist Aleister Crowley (1875-1947), who lived at number 31 in the early '20s.

A Year in London:
Two Things to Do Every Day of the Year

ISBN: 978-1-909282-69-1, 256 pages

David Hampshire

London offers a wealth of things to do, from exuberant festivals and exciting sports events to a plethora of fascinating museums and stunning galleries, from luxury and oddball shops to first-class restaurants and historic pubs, beautiful parks and gardens to pulsating nightlife and clubs. Whatever your interests and tastes, you'll find an abundance of things to enjoy – with a copy of this book you'll never be at a loss for something to do in one of the world's greatest cities.

£11.95

Living and Working in London

ISBN: 978-1-907339-50-9, 6th edition, 336 pages

David Hampshire & Graeme Chesters

Living and Working in London, first published in 2000 and now in its 6th edition, is the most comprehensive book available about daily life – and essential reading for newcomers. What's it really like Living and Working in London? Not surprisingly there's a lot more to life than bobbies, beefeaters and busbys! This book is guaranteed to hasten your introduction to the London way of life, irrespective of whether you're planning to stay for a few months or indefinitely. Adjusting to day to day life in London just got a whole lot simpler!

£14.95

INDEX

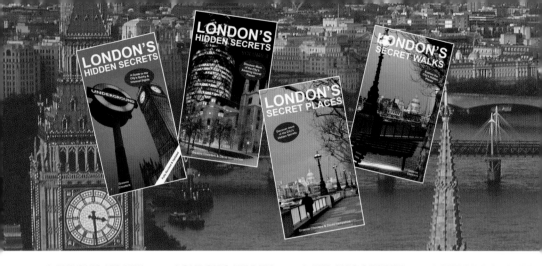